Michael Faulkner

Also by Gavin Lambert

GWTW

GWTW

The Making of GONE WITH THE WIND

by
Gavin Lambert

AN ATLANTIC MONTHLY PRESS BOOK
Little, Brown and Company—Boston—Toronto

SECOND PRINTING

T 10/73

Portions of this book have appeared in *The Atlantic.*

Library of Congress Cataloging in Publication Data

Lambert, Gavin.
    GWTW; the making of Gone with the wind.

    "An Atlantic Monthly Press book."
    Bibliography: p.
    1. Gone With the Wind. [Motion picture]
I. Title.
PN1997.G59L3   791.43'7   73-12081
ISBN 0-316-51284-2

ATLANTIC—LITTLE, BROWN BOOKS
ARE PUBLISHED BY
LITTLE, BROWN AND COMPANY
IN ASSOCIATION WITH
THE ATLANTIC MONTHLY PRESS

*Published simultaneously in Canada by Little, Brown & Company
(Canada) Limited*

PRINTED IN THE UNITED STATES OF AMERICA

To Joan Didion
and John Gregory Dunne

Contents

Acknowledgments

I<small>N WRITING THIS BOOK</small>, I began with the advantage of having known Vivien Leigh and David Selznick; and I had always remembered Vivien Leigh's comments whenever the subject of *GWTW* came up.

When I recorded talks with George Cukor for the book *On Cukor*, his recollections were invaluable. I would also like to thank others involved with *GWTW*, who gave me their time, opinions, and memories: Lee Garmes, who photographed almost a third of it; Olivia de Havilland; Hal Kern, its editor; Raymond Klune, its production manager; and Lydia Schiller, Selznick's production secretary and continuity girl on the picture.

List of Illustrations

one

THE COPPERFIELD CONNECTION

AVID SELZNICK'S FATHER was an adventurer who made and lost his pile in the early days of the film industry, and the son inherited many of his qualities — *chutzpah*, galvanic energy, a taste for gambling and self-display, a hard heart in business and a soft one in personal relations. (The later years of David's career, when he seemed more interested in making deals than making pictures, form an almost eerie parallel to his father's.) The exuberant sharper also bequeathed to his son a reverence for culture and good living. He collected Ming vases and vintage wines, and his favorite book was *David Copperfield*, which the boy began to read at the age of seven.

In one important respect, however, they differed. For the adventurer movies were simply a game, an operation, another field in which to gamble. For David they became a genuine passion, obsessive and strangely methodical; if Mammon was a god, Art was a goddess, and he pursued both with equal fervor.

The act of a child prefigures the future style of a producer. Fascinated by the business his father had taken up, the grammar-school boy began compiling a card index of directors and writers, noting their every success and failure. It became a basic source of reference when, at the age of twenty-nine, he was appointed vice-president of a major Hollywood studio.

Lewis J. Zeleznik, born in Kiev, Russia, in 1870, worked his way to the United States at the age of eighteen. Changing his name to Selznick, he settled in Pittsburgh, where he built up a successful jewelry retail business. In 1910 he overreached himself for the first time when he decided to open "the world's largest jewelry store" in New York. Its doors closed after a few months, and without this modestly grandiose failure there might never have been David's production of *Gone With the Wind*.

For this was the time when many businessmen, most of them Jewish emigrés, were turning to a new business. Louis Bernard Mayer from Minsk, having made some money dealing in scrap metal, used it to buy old theaters which he converted into nickelodeons, thus taking his first step toward becoming the Emperor of MGM. Adolph Zukor, a furrier from Ricse, Hungary, invested his savings in buying the rights to a French four-reeler, *Queen Elizabeth*, starring Sarah Bernhardt, thus taking *his* first step toward the foundation of Paramount Pictures. Sammy Goldfish, a glove salesman from Warsaw, persuaded his brother-in-law Jesse Lasky, who owned a chain of vaudeville houses, to risk a few thousand in film production. They went out to Hollywood, then only a village where no studios had yet been built, and met a young actor-playwright named Cecil B. De Mille. Lasky put his money into *The Squaw Man*, which De Mille was about to shoot in a converted barn; his brother-in-law was appointed producer, and after the film's success Sammy Goldfish decided to be known as Samuel Goldwyn.

Lewis J. Selznick entered the film business through a friend who owned stock in Universal Film Manufacturing and who commissioned Selznick to sell it for him to one of two men engaged in a struggle for control of the company. Appraising the situation, Selznick favored Carl Laemmle from Wurttemberg, Germany, formerly store manager of a clothing company in Wisconsin. (The other candidate, an Irishman named Pat Powers, disappeared soon afterward from the motion picture scene.) By selling Laemmle the stock and enabling him to gain the upper hand at Universal, Selznick maneuvered himself into a job with the company. Another struggle for power soon followed, since both men were too ambitious to remain colleagues for long. While Selznick had great enthusiasm for business intrigue, he was less experienced than Laemmle, who ousted him. Briefly out in the cold, he met a mail order agent named Arthur Spiegel and persuaded him to become a partner in a new company with the flaunty title of World Film Corporation. (The eleven-year-old David was present when this deal was made.) At that time it was the practice of both Laemmle and Zukor to entice "prestige" names from the theater to film their successes, and Selznick followed it. Outbidding his rivals for the services of Clara Kimball Young, Nazimova, Lionel Barrymore and Lillian Russell, he also employed a young director named Allan Dwan, who saw every D. W. Griffith film as it came out and cannily imitated the master's innovations — with such speed that he became the second American director to use the close-up.

After quarreling with Spiegel, Selznick next induced Clara Kimball Young to become his partner. For the next few years he and his rivals stole each other's stars, intriguing endlessly over the Talmadge sisters, tried to buy each other out, feuded in open letters to the trade press, and competed in flamboyant publicity stunts. The climax of these occurred in 1917, when Selznick cabled the deposed Czar Nicholas of Russia, offering him a position with his company. "When I was a boy in Russia your police treated my people very badly but no hard feelings. . . ." There was no reply from the last of the Romanovs.

One empire fell, another expanded. A Rolls Royce, a 22-room apartment on Park Avenue, and the collection of Ming vases became the symbols of Selznick's success. Yet even at its height the operation struck a wrong note, for in the arena of ambition and self-display Selznick was less sophisticated than Laemmle and Zukor, and had the effect of uniting them against him. Compared to the furrier, the glove salesman and the scrap metal merchant, the jewelry dealer seemed an upstart. They waited for him to overreach himself again.

Apart from extravagance, Selznick's greatest mistake was to remain in New York when the trend was West. By the early '20s Laemmle had moved to Hollywood and taken charge of the growing, prosperous Universal lot. Mayer had started producing pictures in a downtown Los Angeles studio rented from a man who made documentaries about animals; the premises included a small zoo containing, symbolically, a lion. Zukor and Lasky had merged to form Paramount. Selznick's stars followed the trend to the West, and he found himself increasingly isolated. In 1923 the company went bankrupt. Since its owner had quarreled with, or otherwise alienated almost everybody, his ruin was greeted with applause.

This time the overreaching was final. There was a last, pathetic attempt to recoup by cashing in on a land boom in Florida. After its failure, Lewis J. Selznick retired from the field. Rolls Royce, apartment, Ming vases, and his wife's jewels were sold, a squadron of servants dismissed. The Jester — as his rivals nicknamed him — moved to a three-room walk-up where Mrs. Selznick did the housework and cooking.

The Jester's naïveté and greed might not in themselves have proved self-destructive. His methods, and the emnity they aroused, had a less forgivable reason behind them. For he never cared about the movies themselves; he was blind to the coin in which he dealt and publicized his contempt for it. In 1917 he told a congressional committee investigating the financial structure of the industry, "Less brains are necessary in the motion picture business than in any other." The movies remained for him on the level of the poker games at which he could win or lose thousands of dollars in a single night. They could never be art, for art was Ming vases and *David Copperfield* and Nazimova in the theater, way beyond the reach of his own canned versions of *Trilby* and *Wildfire*.

The other merchants, the dealers in scrap metal and furs and gloves from Russia and Central Europe, had certainly been attracted to the movies initially for the same reasons as Selznick. There was quick money to be made, and the new entertainment form, being silent, presented no language barrier. (The merchants, who had escaped from their ghettos at twelve or thirteen, had little formal education, and some wrestled with the English language until the end of their lives.) But in the new medium, which had begun as carnival, sideshow, nickelodeon, its promoters gradually discovered something more. Mayer, Goldwyn and the others developed a passion for the movies and saw their extraordinary potential. The passion and the vision might be primitive and narrow, but it was also intense and lasting and in a raw way imaginative. Starting as wheeler-dealers, they realized they had something unique on their hands and turned into founding fathers. Lewis J. Selznick, however, remained a wheeler-dealer all his active life, a promoter for the sake of promotion, and so his downfall is not for mourning and his career chiefly remarkable for its effect on his son.

Or, rather, on two sons. (There was a third, Howard, who never went into the film business.) To Myron, the eldest, and David, born in 1902, their father was a martyr. They loved him deeply, believed him to be a true friend of the artist, and when

7

his empire collapsed they saw him as a victim of callous business-men. He had been his own victim, of course, and artists for him were only people to make money out of, but in the minds of his indignant young sons the legend took hold. In Myron's case it dominated his whole life. David modified his view in later years; he told Kevin Brownlow, author of *The Parade's Gone By*, that his father started out as an enthusiast and then became "too concerned with empire building." There is no hint of conscious irony in this remark.

While he still had money, Lewis Selznick had been generous with it. A lavish spender, he believed he could always earn more, and passed on this attitude — as well as a liberal weekly allowance — to Myron and David. Movie-struck from their schooldays, both brothers left Columbia University to work for their father. After the fall, they were suddenly penniless. In his autobiography, *A Child of the Century*, Ben Hecht remembers Myron and David Selznick "zigzagging through the town to throw the creditors off the scent." Myron went out to Hollywood, and David followed after raising enough money to produce a couple of shorts, one about boxing and the other of Rudolph Valentino judging a beauty contest.

In Hollywood the brothers had the advantage of being brought up in the business, but the disadvantage of Selznick's personal unpopularity and failure. However, their determination to succeed was unbeatable. Within a few years Myron had established himself as the most powerful agent in town; more than that, he revolutionized the whole technique of agenting. Until that time, agents had had little power and less social standing. Starting with a few clients, mainly personal friends such as Lewis Milestone and William Wellman, Myron built up a company that by the early '30s handled at least 50 percent of Hollywood's most famous stars, directors, and writers, and set the pattern for the later power structures of MCA and its imitators. A driven, possessed man who drank heavily, he believed he had a mission to revenge artists on the producers who had ruined his father. "His work of vengeance changed the Hollywood climate," Hecht wrote in A Child of the Century. "It doubled and quadrupled the salaries of directors, writers and actors — myself among them. . . . Brooding in his tent after a sortie on a major studio, Myron would chortle, 'I'll break them all. I'll send all those thieves and fourflushers crawling to the poorhouse. Before I'm done the artists in this town will have all the money.' " Before he was done (he died in 1944 of an internal hemorrhage), they certainly had a great deal of it.

David's rise was no less spectacular, though ironically enough he became a producer, in Myron's eyes the enemy profession. (Myron and he remained closely attached even so, but brotherhood was never allowed to interfere with business. Making a deal, Myron was as tough with David as with all the others.) Equally possessed, David had the greater equilibrium. Born with the sun in Taurus (the sign of the Builder and Producer), he seems to have combined his father's quicksilver arrogance with the traditional Taurean staying power and love of organization. Shortly after his arrival in California he made a characteristic move. Because his own name coincided with that of an uncle he disliked, and because it struck him as insufficiently impressive for the impression he wished to make, he decided it needed a middle initial — like his father, like Louis B. Mayer, like Cecil B. De Mille — and settled on O as the most imposing. (He announced that it stood for Oliver; but O in itself represents Omega, the end, the climax, the last of its kind.) It certainly seems to have imposed. By 1931 he had brought off two major coups: he married Irene, the daughter of Louis B. Mayer (over her father's strong opposition — "He'll end up a bum just like his old man!") and became vice-president in charge of production at RKO.

When Selznick took over, RKO was short of prestige and profits, but within a year he had revitalized it in both areas. His first step was to approve Merian C. Cooper's *King Kong*, a project that had been hanging fire; his second was to pick a subject that he would produce himself. To direct *What Price Hollywood?* he chose George Cukor, whom he'd met when both were new to California, and had introduced to a Russian friend, Lewis Milestone. Cukor had worked as dialogue director on *All Quiet on the Western Front*, and was then signed to make films for Paramount. The Hollywood story, conceived as a vehicle for the fading Clara Bow, then retailored for the rising Constance Bennett, was, as Cukor said later, "dear to David's heart. He later used it in a different way for the first version of *A Star Is Born*. Like the audience at that time, Selznick had a very romantic view of Hollywood, a real love of it. . . . Most of the other Hollywood pictures make it a kind of crazy, kooky place, but to David it was absolutely real, he believed in it." At that time, of course, it was a heady place in which to believe. The rise of Selznick coincided with the rise of the great studios. He stood at the entrance to an age of triumphant prosperity, unrivaled arsenals of technical resources and international talent that entertained the world. And yet, curiously enough, David's two films about Hollywood were preoccupied with failure. In the story dear to his heart, while the movie queen survives, the male figure — in *What Price Hollywood?* a director, in *A Star Is Born* an actor — becomes a drunken failure and commits suicide. While Myron's heavy drinking may or may not have had a bearing on this, it seems certain that for all his romantic love of the place, Selznick was not blind to the insecurities beneath its alluring surface.

On one level the '30s were the great "halcyon period," as S. N. Behrman (who worked on several scripts in Hollywood, including *Anna Karenina* for Selznick) writes in his memoir, *People in a Diary*. "There were few places in America where you could go out to dinner with Harpo and Groucho Marx, the Franz Werfels, Leopold Stokowski, Aldous Huxley, Somerset Maugham, and George and Ira Gershwin." On another and less obvious level, there was a ruthless attitude toward failure and constant, secret intrigue within the higher echelons of power. Falls from grace could be as drastic as rises to favor. Behrman tells the story of how Lubitsch learned one morning that he'd been dismissed as head of Paramount from his gym instructor, who had massaged a studio executive the night before and heard the gossip. Selznick's energy and ambition were outstanding even in a place bursting with both qualities; but perhaps, like others, he was propelled by fear as well as enthusiasm. The world in which he'd chosen to succeed also gave back echoes of his father's failure.

What Price Hollywood? was greatly liked by both the critics and the public and led to further collaborations between Selznick and Cukor. A *Bill of Divorcement* introduced Katharine Hepburn to the screen and began a director–star partnership that became famous. For all three the pinnacle of this period was *Little Women*, a piece of classic Americana unequaled for intimate, charming exactness.

Selznick's success at RKO reconciled him, on the business level at least, with his father-in-law. Mayer had been quarreling repeatedly with the second vice-president of MGM, the fragile but determined Irving Thalberg. After Thalberg recovered from a heart attack and left for a long European vacation with his wife, Norma Shearer, the Emperor made overtures to Selznick, offering him carte blanche as producer at the studio and implying he might soon take Thalberg's place. Selznick accepted, not out of affection for Mayer, nor because he wanted to succeed Thalberg, but the resources of Hollywood's most glamorous and celebrated studio were irresistible. He left RKO in 1933. Cukor went with him, and they made the all-star *Dinner at Eight*. Based on a Broadway hit, with a cast including Marie Dressler, John and Lionel Barrymore, Jean Harlow, Wallace Beery, and Billie Burke, it had the same formula as Thalberg's coup of the previous year, *Grand Hotel*. Adept from his experience in the theater, Cukor handled the line-up of sacred monsters with ease and skill, shot the whole blockbuster in twenty-seven days, and made of it one of the most hard-edged of Depression comedies.

The film earned a lot of money, gained Selznick more prestige in the industry than he'd ever enjoyed before, and killed the joke heard everywhere when he joined MGM — "the son-in-law also rises." Other successes quickly followed — *Dancing Lady*, with Clark Gable and Joan Crawford, which introduced Astaire to the screen; *Manhattan Melodrama*, again with Gable; and *Viva Villa* — and Selznick found himself in a position to achieve something he'd wanted for a long time: a real cultural splash. As a work of literature *Little Women* was at best a minor classic, and the film itself, for all its virtues, on a small scale. Selznick was now, as they say, thinking big. He had already prepared for the occasion by compiling a methodical, obsessive list of all the classics he might one day wish to film. At the head of the list was *David Copperfield*, his father's favorite novel. He chose Cukor to direct. Mayer opposed the project, fearful that classics were bad box-office (and the record showed that most of them were); when his son-in-law insisted, he tried to impose the MGM child star, Jackie Cooper, for the young David. Selznick and Cukor held out for an unknown and discovered Freddie Bartholemew in England.

Producer and director agreed that the way to film Dickens was not to restructure him, nor to add new and more "commercial" elements to the story, but to respect his massively episodic style and concentrate on the gallery of characters. For the time this was an almost revolutionary approach, and unnerved the studio even further, especially since it would involve a movie about two and a half hours long. Box-office insurance was taken out by assembling an all-star cast for the other major roles — W. C. Fields, Maureen O'Sullivan, Lionel Barrymore, Basil Rathbone, Edna May Oliver, and all — but the audience reaction at a sneak preview in Bakersfield was discouraging. Selznick toyed with the idea of eliminating Barrymore as Daniel Peggoty (in fact, the only weak performance), then shrewdly decided to avoid the wrath of Dickens-lovers and trim the running time by a few minutes instead. When *David Copperfield* was released, both critics and public liked it very much — rightly so, for in spite of some uncertain art direction it has great vitality and conviction, and remains the most authentically flavored Dickens movie ever made. Later, David confessed that with a mixture of sentiment and superstition, during the preparation and shooting of the film, "I lugged with me every place we went the old-fashioned red leather copy of *Copperfield* which my father had given me."

This success was a turning point in Selznick's career, for it proved not only that a film of a classic novel could make money, but that respect for the original paid off. Now firmly launched on the road to prestige, he consulted his list again and repeated the formula with *Anna Karenina*, for Garbo, and *A Tale of Two Cities*. By this time Thalberg had recovered and returned to the studio. Having no wish to be entangled in Mayer's intrigues, Selznick declared that he was leaving to form his own company. The Emperor alternately threatened and made promises, but the son-in-law had been laying plans for a year while working out his contract. Studio politics apart, the young producer now wanted to run his own organization. In a memo to Nicholas Schenck, the president of MGM, he explained with that characteristic touch of portentousness: "I am at a crossroads where a sign hangs high — 'To thine own self be true, and it must follow, as the night the day, thou canst not then be false to any man.'"

Assembling a formidable list of stockholders, he announced the formation of Selznick International Pictures at the end of 1935. Capitalized at over $3,000,000, it had the millionaire John Hay ("Jock") Whitney, whom he'd originally met through Merian C. Cooper of *King Kong*, as chairman of the board; the directors included Cornelius Whitney and three Whitney sisters, representing an investment of $2,400,000, three New York financiers, Robert Lehman, and Arthur and John Hertz ($150,000 each), Myron Selznick ($200,000), and as a gesture of private sympathy, a silent investment of $200,000 from Irving and Norma Shearer Thalberg. Mayer felt deeply rejected, and the event was to have repercussions when David came to produce *Gone With the Wind*.

The old Pathé studio in Culver City became the new headquarters. A portrait of Lewis J. Selznick hung on the wall of his son's office. From the beginning "class" was the watchword, and both the Venus de Milo and the Winged Victory were considered for company trademarks. Then Selznick was struck one day by the facade of the studio building. Colonial in style, with white pillars, it seems now to carry an unconscious premonition of the movie rendering of Margaret Mitchell's Tara, as prophetic as the adopted O. Superimposed on this emblem was the proud slogan, "In a Tradition of Quality."

The Tradition began with adaptations of *Little Lord Fauntleroy*, *The Garden of Allah* (Selznick's one failure, but interestingly bizarre) , and *The Prisoner of Zenda*. This list of "classics" suggests that his literary taste was basically nineteenth-century-romantic, and erratic at that, but for Dickens and Robert Hichens alike he advertised the same unwavering, serious respect. A compiler of lists is also a natural composer of notes and memos. In a series of them, written while he was making *Anna Karenina*, he outlined his procedure for adapting a classic:

Having just gone through the difficulties of adapting *David Copperfield*, the prospect of compressing Tolstoy's work without too great a loss of values did not faze us. . . . Our first blow was a flat refusal by the Hays office to permit the entire section of the story dealing with Anna's illegitimate child . . . but even what remained of the personal story of Anna seemed so far superior to such inventions of writers today as could be considered possibilities for Miss Garbo. . . . We had to eliminate everything that could even remotely be classified as a passionate love scene, and we had to make it perfectly clear that not merely did Anna suffer but that Vronsky suffered. . . . Our next step in the adaptation was to decide which of the several stories that are told in the book we could tell on the screen without diverting the audience's interest from one line to another. This meant the minimizing of the story of Levin, including that magnificent scene, the death of Levin's brother. . . . From this point on it became a matter of the careful selection and editing of Tolstoy's scenes, with a surprisingly little amount of original writing necessary. . . . I like to think that we retained the literary quality and the greater part of the poignant story of a woman torn between two equal loves and doomed to tragedy whichever one she chose."

The tone of this note, and the memo habit that was to grow over the years, stretching into hundreds of thousands of words, provide a clue to something which happened within Selznick at the time. The stilted style, rather like an old-fashioned politician's and rich with doublethink, is both curiously old for a man still in his early thirties and masterly in its technique of self-justification — the glossing over at the end of the difference between fidelity and distortion with "I like to think . . ." These are statements in the form of an order, and the order comes from the top. He has found the secret of authority, which is belief in oneself at all times. A parallel can be seen in the increasing size and grandeur of the films themselves, which also cost more to produce — starting with *Fauntleroy* at about $550,000 and rising to *Zenda* at about $900,000.

Another habit now on the increase was gambling. Selznick liked to play mainly at a club on the Sunset Strip, and was dedicated but unlucky at roulette. He had a system, of course, devised as elaborately as the card index and the lists and the memos, but it seldom seemed to work. And in one night of poker he lost over $100,000 to Joseph Schenck, chairman of the board of Twentieth Century-Fox. He also built a house in Beverly Hills for himself and Irene, furnished with expensive antiques, a dining table that seated thirty, and a projection room. Servants were employed around the clock, as were secretaries, in case he wished to eat or dictate in the small hours. Dinner parties for the Hollywood elite and occasional weekend yachting excursions were planned like productions. The after-dinner movie started promptly at the scheduled time, and invitations to the yacht arrived in the form of sailing orders.

From poker to life-style to movies, the stakes were growing higher.

Early in 1936 Selznick's story editor on the East Coast, Kay Brown, sent him a long synopsis of a long forthcoming novel. It was called *Gone With the Wind,* and nobody had ever heard of the author. Kay Brown felt strongly enough about its possibilities to end her note of recommendation, "I know that after you read the book you will drop everything and buy it."

He didn't. Although he read the digest at once, and on the face of it the project should have seemed irresistible — a twentieth-century work with all the nineteenth-century romantic ingredients he adored — Selznick resisted. While the nostalgia and sweep of the material intrigued him, his business sense made signals of alarm. Pictures about the Civil War, with the exception of *Birth of a Nation* — and that was a long time ago — had never been successful at the box office. Only the previous year *So Red the Rose*, directed by his friend King Vidor with the popular stars Margaret Sullavan and Randolph Scott, had confirmed the jinx all over again. A cabled memo to Kay Brown ended, "MOST SORRY TO HAVE TO SAY NO IN FACE OF YOUR ENTHUSIASM FOR THIS STORY."

A few days later, Selznick began to have second thoughts. In another cabled memo to Kay Brown he agreed that the novel had great possibilities, especially if filmed in color; but he was worried about the difficulty of casting the leads, and the high asking price for the rights — $65,000. Torn between enthusiasm and doubt for six weeks, he made no final move. In the Hollywood phrase, he sat on it — "it" being the symbolic toilet seat which one can decide neither to use nor to leave. But Kay Brown was sure of her instinct (and with good reason: a few years later she recommended to Selznick another unpublished novel, *Rebecca*). She sent the synopsis of *Gone With the Wind* to the company chairman, Jock Whitney. His response was immediate, and he told her that if Selznick didn't buy the rights, he would go after them himself. This had its effect. Selznick made an offer of $50,000.

To the end of her life Margaret Mitchell remained aloof from the movies. She enjoyed going to them, but had no desire to become involved with their world. According to a member of her family, she accepted Selznick's offer "because Macmillan Company, her publishers, through the agent Annie Laurie Williams, advised that it was the best offer she would get." Beyond that, she had seen *David Copperfield*, admired it, and felt that her work could not be in safer hands.

two

RESULTS OF AN ACCIDENT

THE TWO GREATEST EVENTS in Margaret Mitchell's life, the writing of *Gone With the Wind* and her death, occurred by accident. As a child she loved to ride horseback, but a bad fall permanently weakened her left ankle. In 1926 she was still living in her birthplace, Atlanta, was four feet eleven inches tall and as old as the century, married for the second time to an advertising executive named John Marsh, and walking on crutches, after violently spraining her damaged ankle. She was living the life of a semi-cripple, who had been writing since she was six years old with slight visible results (four years on the Atlanta *Journal*; a handful of short stories never offered for publication; an abandoned novel dealing with the Jazz Age). It is probable that she would have given up writing altogether if Marsh had not believed in her talent and applied pressure at a telling moment.

There seemed no way out of trying again. As long as the ankle refused to heal her social life was curtailed; she was unable to dance, which she loved, and the days were reduced to reading and playing bridge. Most of all, it would please her husband. So one morning she limped to her typewriter and began writing a novel about the Civil War. Until she was ten years old, she hadn't even known that the South had lost it. Her mother took her on a buggy ride, showed her the surviving ruins of gutted plantations in the countryside beyond Atlanta, and then broke the important news. Later she said that the moment haunted her, this tale of defeat while she gazed at skeletons of the past, and the War itself continued to cast a shadow across her life. She grew up in a city where memories of it, through people and places, were still vivid. Another journey that lingered in her mind was a visit to some relatives on a farm twenty miles south of Atlanta; it had belonged to her grand-aunts, who had escaped there on the last train out of Atlanta before Sherman arrived.

When she began the novel she knew only the beginning and end of the story, and wrote the last chapter first: Rhett Butler walking out on Scarlett. In fact she hardly ever wrote in continuity, skipping between events that took place years apart and storing each chapter in a large manila envelope. As time passed, the envelopes faded and became blotched with coffee stains. On some of them she scribbled kitchen recipes and grocery lists. Lack of confidence made her secretive; she allowed only her husband to read the work in progress, but disclosed something about it to a close friend, Lois Cole, who later went to New York to work for the Macmillan publishing house. The rest of her friends knew that something was up, because a visitor would arrive unexpectedly from time to time and catch her hobbling to hide a bulky envelope underneath a cushion on the sofa. No questions were asked because they'd always considered Peggy Marsh a mystery, and she had an aura of privacy that people instinctively respected. A Roman Catholic, she had divorced her first husband after a few months, and married his best man. Uncommunicative about herself, she was a lively conversationalist on many other topics. "If you want your dinner party to be a success," said a friend, "invite Peggy Marsh." After the novel came out, many people said that she looked like Melanie Hamilton but in person was really much closer to Scarlett. This displeased her. The tiny, soberly dressed lady always insisted that Scarlett was "a far from admirable character."

Her heroine began as Pansy O'Hara, a character from one of the unpublished stories; Melanie was at first called Permelia, then Melisande; and when she'd been writing for about a year Fontenoy Hall became Tara. This accidental, haphazard method continued for two more years, with alternate versions of several episodes adding to the pile of manila envelopes. (How to kill off Scarlett's second husband, Frank Kennedy, was not finally solved until a few months before publication.) For a few scenes, it is clear she drew from personal experience. In 1918, while she was away at Smith College in Massachusetts, her mother died during a flu epidemic in Atlanta; in the novel, Scarlett returns to Tara and learns that her mother has died of typhoid. Earlier that same year she became engaged to a young lieutenant who went to France and was killed there, just as Scarlett's first husband goes off to war and loses his life (less heroically) right after their marriage. In 1919 she scandalized Atlanta society by performing an exotic Apache dance at a party organized for charity by local debutantes. No well-brought-up girl was expected to behave like this so soon after her mother's death, and *Gone With the Wind* echoes the situation when Scarlett appalls everybody by dancing with Rhett in her widow's black at the Atlanta Bazaar. In 1917 a major fire broke out in her native city, and she worked all night at a panic-stricken emergency center. For Scarlett's escape from a burning, terrified Atlanta she no doubt consulted her memories as well as the history books.

By 1930 the novel was about two-thirds finished and the manila envelopes concealed over a thousand typewritten pages. It still lacked an opening chapter, several connecting passages, and a title. She hesitated between *Another Day, Bugles Sang*

True, Not in Our Stars, and *Tote the Weary Load,* not really satisfied with any of them. And by this time the weary load itself was beginning to get her down. Her ankle finally healed, and she could escape back to the social life, country club luncheons, dinner parties, and dances.

When the Marshes moved to a new apartment she stored all the envelopes in a closet. From time to time, she worked at trying to finish the book, but it was largely in response to pressure from her husband; the original impetus seems to have been lost. "I hit the book a few more licks in 1930 and 1931. . . ." She developed a curious, maddening indifference to the enormous amount of work she'd already done, and five years later the novel was still incomplete, the envelopes fading in the closet. In 1934 she hardly hit the book any licks at all, since her neck was in a brace after an automobile accident. In April 1935, Harold Latham of the Macmillan Company was visiting Atlanta. He knew about the novel through Peggy Marsh's old friend, Lois Cole, now an associate editor and his colleague. ("If she can write the way she talks," said Lois Cole, "it should be a honey.") Latham met her at a country club luncheon and asked to see the manuscript. "I have no novel," she told him, surprised and alarmed, but her husband persuaded her to take it to Latham's hotel next day. Summoned to the lobby, he saw the tiny lady sitting on a divan beside the biggest manuscript he'd ever encountered in his life, the pile of envelopes reaching to her shoulders. "Take the thing before I change my mind," she said, and was gone again.

After buying a suitcase to carry the mass of envelopes, Latham began reading the novel on the train to New Orleans. Physically it was one of the most discouraging manuscripts ever offered to him, the pages now yellowed and moldering, the typescript covered with pencil corrections. A cable awaited him at his hotel in New Orleans: "SEND THE MANUSCRIPT BACK HAVE CHANGED MY

MIND." Ignoring it, he continued reading the work on the train to New York; in spite of the gaps and the rough, unrevised quality of parts of the writing, and the sheer difficulty of reading the aged, untidy pages, he sniffed a best seller. He made an immediate offer to publish the book — if only she would finish it. Astonished, she said to her husband, "I don't see how they can make heads or tails of it." Then she worried about how the South would receive the book if she allowed it to be published. If Atlanta disapproved, wouldn't she be socially ostracized? Marsh cajoled her into accepting the offer, then both he and Latham pressured her to work for another six months, during which she checked all the historical details, rewrote the opening chapter several times, decided that Frank Kennedy should meet his death as a result of joining the Ku Klux Klan, and finally found her title in a poem by Ernest Dowson, *Cynara*.

Macmillan scheduled the publication of *Gone With the Wind* for May 1936, deciding to print 10,000 copies priced at $3. Then the Book-of-the-Month Club wanted the novel for its July selection. The publication date was delayed accordingly, and 50,000 more copies printed. By the end of July it was clear that a phenomenon had occurred. The *New York Times* gave the novel an enthusiastic front-page review in its book section; the *New York Sun* compared it to *War and Peace*; Stephen Vincent Benét, Robert Nathan and a visiting H. G. Wells endorsed it; and the entire southern press quieted its author's fears with a chorus of praise. Within six months half a million copies had been sold, and the figure more than doubled within a year. In 1937 it was awarded the Pulitzer Prize. Even the less amiable reviewers, the left-wing papers that accused it of glorifying slavery, the critics like Malcolm Cowley and Louis Kronenberger who found it indifferently written, had to admit its extraordinary impact and the appeal of its passionate escapism.

Now that the reputation of the novel is so tied up with that of the film, it's almost impossible to write about them separately. One thing is clear, however; because of the figure of Scarlett O'Hara, the overwhelming effect of *Gone With the Wind* in 1936 was on women. As a work of literature it is no better and no worse than most best sellers, but it struck a deep emotional chord, rather as the immensely superior *Jane Eyre* had done in England almost a hundred years earlier. Charlotte Brontë's heroine was the first emancipated young lady, determined to assert her independence in the face of social pressures, in Victorian fiction. Not beautiful, but sensual, not rich, but intelligent and strong-willed, her relationship with men was a duel. The emotional point she made to women readers was resistance to male domination. Scarlett O'Hara is a glamorized version of the same idea. Attractive, spoiled, selfish, she can still act like a man in moments of crisis, and even though Rhett Butler walks out on her at the end, it's not certain that she won't get him back. In any case she's a survivor, and her unbroken spirit continued the revolution that Charlotte Brontë began. "I still feebly say," Margaret Mitchell wrote to a friend, "that it's just a simple story of some people who went up and some who went down, those who could take it and those who couldn't." Her Scarlett could take it, and for thousands of women she raised the basic question of exactly what "independence" involved and how high the stakes should be raised.

Her effect on her creator, Peggy Marsh of Atlanta, born Margaret Mitchell, remains ironic and a little sad. By writing *Gone With the Wind* she struck her own blow for women's independence, but it was reluctant and painful and would never have been sustained without her husband's help. Fame and fortune, when they arrived, seemed more a threat than a liberation. She retreated even further into provincial married life and never wrote anything more. "I'm on the run," she wrote soon after the novel came out. "I'm sure Scarlett O'Hara never struggled to get out of Atlanta or suffered more during her siege of Atlanta than I have suffered during the siege that has been on since publication day." She contemplated a play about the effects of celebrity on a couple like herself and John Marsh, but never came to grips with it. Acclaim did nothing to heal her basic lack of self-confidence. The limelight stunned her; she refused to go to Hollywood to meet Selznick and would have nothing to do with the production of the movie; she was nervous at public appearances and eventually declined to be photographed, since it would only expose her to further recognition.

In 1945 her husband had a heart attack from which he never completely recovered, and Scarlett's creator became more Melanie-like than ever, patient nurse as well as devoted wife. In 1949, while crossing a street in Atlanta with John Marsh, she was hit by a speeding car and died five days later, a few months away from her forty-ninth birthday. Marsh survived until 1952, and was buried beside her in Oakland Cemetery, Atlanta.

Fifteen years later tourists were still arriving every day to see Margaret Mitchell's grave, and occasional pilgrims make the journey even now. A cemetery attendant reported that many of them were disappointed to find only a bare, unassuming head-stone with nothing to single it out from the hundreds of others. It remains the only formal memorial to this perplexingly private woman, who requested Marsh to burn the basic manuscript of *Gone With the Wind* after her death. All that survives of it is a batch of tattered typewritten pages with some penciled cor-rections, and the final edited proof — just enough to show that she really wrote the book.

three

THE SECOND BURNING OF ATLANTA

H IS OFFER FOR THE RIGHTS of *Gone With the Wind* accepted, Selznick went to Hawaii for a vacation with his wife, and started to read the novel he'd bought. He returned to find it a runaway best seller and already part of the national psyche.

At this point he'd made only one definite decision: that George Cukor should direct the picture. Circumstances propelled him quickly into making another. Thousands of letters from readers and movie fans were arriving at the company's office, and 99 percent of them demanded that Clark Gable play the part of Rhett Butler. Gable was also Selznick's first choice, but he had reasons for not making a move at this moment. The star was under exclusive contract to MGM, and Selznick's relations with his father-in-law were approaching another crisis.

Early in September 1936, Irving Thalberg caught pneumonia. He died two weeks later, and the Emperor at once made new overtures to Selznick, this time a firm offer to succeed him as second vice-president of MGM. Always jealous of his son-in-law, piqued that he'd made a success of independence, he now wanted the victory of a return to the fold. More than this, although he publicly scoffed at *Gone With the Wind,* saying it would be impossibly expensive and an insane risk, the seasoned professional suspected that David had pulled off the coup of the year. He wanted to play vice-president in charge of production to his young rival's second vice-president, and he wanted *Gone With the Wind* for MGM.

Fully aware of the stakes, Selznick at first postponed the game. He turned down Mayer's offer, explaining that he wanted to continue running his own company. Mayer then suggested that MGM would be interested in buying *Gone With the Wind* anyway, with David as producer. The Gable situation was not mentioned; cunningly, the Emperor talked only of his casting ideas for the other leading parts — Joan Crawford as Scarlett, Maureen O'Sullivan as Melanie, and Melvyn Douglas as Ashley. Selznick said he'd have to think about it. Knowing it was only a matter of time before his son-in-law came back to him, Mayer waited. It was the kind of power play at which he was adept. ("My son-in-law is one stubborn fool. I'll get even with him.") Meanwhile, Selznick began exploring other possibilities for Rhett. Gary Cooper had already occurred to him, and he approached Sam Goldwyn, to whom the actor was under contract. Goldwyn unequivocally refused to loan him out. Selznick next thought of Errol Flynn, the movies' top swashbuckler since *Captain Blood* and *The Charge of the Light Brigade,* and under contract to Warner Brothers. This time he was offered a package instead of a refusal. Bette Davis, also the property of Warners', had begun an ardent campaign for the role of Scarlett, and Jack Warner was prepared to make her part of the deal. Selznick was tempted, but Davis was not: desperate though she might be, she wouldn't play Scarlett to Flynn's Rhett. (Her reward for this failure to compromise was that Warner forced her into three pictures with Flynn over the next few years.)

Going through the other names most frequently mentioned

in the letters, Selznick found that Warner Baxter had strong support from his native South; but he was too old, and lacking in sex appeal. Incredibly, Basil Rathbone had a sizeable percentage of the remaining 1 percent, but Selznick dismissed this idea as well. Ronald Colman, under contract to the company, had come up in previous discussions with Kay Brown. In her first excitement over the book she had called Colman long-distance and read him a few passages. "Ripping!" said the actor. "Oh, it's topping, absolutely topping!" Implacably British, he was really out of the question, but the fan magazines for a while took up his cause. When interviewed, he always replied that he thought Gable would be a better choice. (There is no record that Colman was ever considered for Ashley — perhaps the physical contrast with Gable would not have been strong enough — but he could certainly have mastered a southern accent as well as Leslie Howard, and might have been a more interesting choice.) Reluctantly, Selznick had to admit that Gable was a necessity. As the Emperor had predicted, he went back to MGM.

The terms were not unexpectedly stiff. MGM would lend Gable at a figure considerably above his usual salary, and provide half the financing (estimated then at $2,500,000), in return for the world distribution rights through its parent company, Loew's, Inc., and half of the total profits.

Mayer knew, of course, that he had the power for a shake-down. His son-in-law needed not only Gable, but money. Selznick had been insistent about protecting the identity of *Gone With the Wind* as a production of his own company, and shooting it on his own lot; but while most of the Selznick International Pictures had shown good profits, the company was not yet breaking even and the stockholders had received no dividends. Turning out only two or three productions a year, each supervised by Selznick with an increasingly fanatical attention to detail, its overheads demanded that the profit from each picture be reinvested in the next. One of the Whitney sisters, Mrs. Charles S. Payson, told a friend that she simply didn't understand the motion picture business. "Everyone assures me that Mr. Selznick's pictures are the best, and that they make the most money, but I've never received a dollar of return." In fact, with three pictures in various stages of production at the time he went back to MGM, Selznick did not have enough capital to make *Gone With the Wind* on his own.

"My son-in-law is one smart fellow," said Mayer when he heard that Selznick had accepted the terms. The only problem was that Gable at first refused the part. Always lacking in confidence, and with a habit of initially turning down roles that proved to be among his most successful (*Mutiny on the Bounty* and *It Happened One Night*), he was frankly terrified at the prospect of Rhett Butler. The fact that he had been cast by popular vote only increased his alarm. "Too big an order," he told Selznick, "I don't want any part of him," and suggested Ronald Colman. But by the terms of his contract with MGM he was in no position to turn down the role unless he went on suspension, and for private reasons this was no time to risk unemployment. Money, as so often in the movies, was the deciding factor. Gable was still married to, though separated from, a Texas matron seventeen years older than himself; he had just fallen in love with Carole Lombard and they wanted to marry. Rhea Langham Gable was determined to exact vengeance by demanding an enormous divorce settlement; and, like Mayer with Selznick, she knew that she had the power for a shakedown. Her lawyers were already mentioning a figure of almost $300,000, a heartache for anyone to part with and a tragedy for a naturally frugal man. On salary to MGM at $4,000 a week (the additional money demanded by Mayer for his services on *Gone With the Wind* would all go to the studio), he needed financial assistance from his employers. So, after protracted negotiations that were really a series of legal blackmails, with MGM and Mrs. Gable as the winners, he signed for the part.

The delay was less important than it seemed, for the deal with MGM meant that Selznick would have to hold up production of the picture for at least two years. Since his company had a contract with United Artists to distribute all his pictures until the end of 1938, *Gone With the Wind* could not be released by MGM until after that time. The real problem, knowing that he could secure Gable and delight an anxious public, was how to keep that public's interest in the project alive.

Out of this dilemma came the idea of a nationwide talent search to find an unknown to play Scarlett O'Hara. When he thought of it, Selznick was certainly not convinced that he *wanted* an unknown — even after shooting began he was still considering stars for the lead — and the search in the end yielded nothing except a girl in Charleston, Alicia Rhett, to play the part of India Wilkes, Ashley's unpleasant sister. But as an attention-getting device it was brilliant. Soon after founding Selznick International he had met Russell Birdwell, a reporter for the Los Angeles *Examiner*. Detecting in him a real flair for news-making and a heartening absence of shame, he appointed Birdwell head of publicity for the company. The news-maker responded with predictable enthusiasm to the idea of a widely publicized hunt for a girl to play the most popular heroine of the decade. Trumpeted by a press conference, three talent executives were picked to cover the country — Charles Morrison was assigned to the West, Oscar Serlin to the North and East, and Max Arnow to the South. Cukor himself accompanied Arnow to the most likely place, after all, to find a Scarlett.

The search received a gratifyingly wide national coverage and was the subject of editorials from the *Times* of Los Angeles to the *Times* of New York. Today, when the casting of unknowns in leading roles is hardly revolutionary, it seems almost inconceivable that such a simple ploy should have worked so well and for so long. But Selznick was handling a very special property at a time when the *mystique* of Hollywood and the star system was at its height. The formation of the Rome–Berlin axis, the Moscow spy trials, the German occupation of Austria and the Munich Conference were comparatively minor events to an isolationist public holding its breath while 1,400 candidates were interviewed and 90 tested as potential flesh and blood of an instant legend. More than this, Selznick and Birdwell were promising the reenactment of a myth dear to the American heart: the sudden rise from rags to riches, from obscurity to honor, and "overnight stardom" was one of the most cherished fantasies of the vast movie public, even though it occurred far less frequently than imagined.

The cost of the whole operation was finally estimated at $92,000, including the tests, of which 149,000 feet were shot in black-and-white and 13,000 feet in Technicolor, a total of more than 24 hours' running time. Later, and privately, both Selznick and Cukor admitted that the results were simply awful. Only during the last few months of the two-year search did columnists and Hollywood colleagues begin to comment rather acidly on the lack of substance behind the glare of spotlights. There were hints that the role was uncastable and the film might never be made. Selznick dealt with this by writing open letters to the columnists, among them the powerful Ed Sullivan, explaining why the film could not be released before 1939 and promising that "the best Scarlett that shows up by the time Gable is available to start work will play the role, willy-nilly."

The most publicized and richly absurd moment of the search occurred on Christmas Day 1937. An outsize package was delivered to Selznick's home by liveried messengers. Ribbons and paper were ripped away to disclose a replica of the novel in its dust jacket, out of which stepped a young girl in crinolines.

"Merry Christmas, Mr. Selznick! I am your Scarlett O'Hara!" When Birdwell gave the story to the press, he was accused of having staged the incident himself. One incident that was certainly not staged was the invasion of Cukor's sleeping car when his train reached Atlanta. A group of hysterical southern belles, some of them in costume, stormed the corridor shrieking for attention and a contract. The most determined of them, known locally as Honey Chile, pursued him unsuccessfully as far as New Orleans.

Not surprisingly, the possibility that an unknown might be chosen to play Scarlett also had its effect on the stars and their fan clubs. As in the case of Gable and Rhett Butler, letters poured in from all over the country — from Europe, too, since the novel was repeating its triumph there — suggesting almost every leading lady of the moment. Many of the ladies suggested themselves. An only halfway satirical article in *Photoplay* noted that "actresses who have never been South of the Slot in San Francisco or below Twenty-third Street in Manhattan, whose closest tie to Dixie in fact, is a faint resemblance to Virginia ham, wander around calling people 'Honey' in a languid, molasses manner." Of the write-ins, Bette Davis was easily the most popular candidate, with 40 percent of the vote, but her refusal to play opposite Flynn had taken her out of the running. The loss of the role haunted her for years. In the 1920's, when Cukor ran a stock company in Rochester, New York, he had employed her for one season, then let her go because there were no more parts he considered suitable for her. In Davis's mind the idea became fixed that he never liked her and had always favored Katharine Hepburn for the role. At late as the '60s she gave out interviews saying that if Cukor had really wanted her, a deal could have been made with Warners' excluding Flynn; and in her autobiography, *The Lonely Life* (1962), she insisted, "His thumbs were down. By such intangibles are careers affected."

Cukor has never been able to understand this. "Imagine," he commented to me, "since she became this great tragedienne and important person, I've been constantly reading that she was fired by George Cukor! And I'd really been awfully kind to her."

The long obsession reveals Davis's inconsolable desire for the part — which was indirectly rewarded. Discovering a story whose southern heroine had obvious affinities with Scarlett, she persuaded Jack Warner to let her make it in 1938. The year before *Gone With the Wind* was a candidate for awards, she won her second Oscar for *Jezebel*, to Selznick's considerable annoyance.

Katharine Hepburn, her imagined downfall, was in fact a self-announced contender, one of several stars who either suggested themselves to Selznick for the role or put their agents to work. Because of her association with both Cukor and Selznick, she was thought for a while to have the inside track; but although Cukor was receptive, Selznick doubted whether she had the sex appeal to enthrall Rhett Butler for so many years, and was worried because at the time motion picture exhibitors were labeling her "box-office poison." He offered to test her, however; but she refused. In Cukor's mind she remained a strong possibility, and he thought that if the search should fail to yield an "ideal" Scarlett, Selznick would reconsider. Then, for a heady day or two, it seemed as if Hepburn had been endorsed by Margaret Mitchell herself. Sternly refusing all invitations to become involved with the production, the author had declined to line up southern belles for Cukor and Arnow in Atlanta, or to state any preference for an actress to play her heroine. But one day, when asked by Mrs. Ogden Reid her opinion of Hepburn, she said "I enjoyed her in *Little Women*, and thought she looked very pretty in hoop skirts." The remark somehow reached a reporter on the Atlanta *Journal*, which printed a story that Hepburn was Margaret Mitchell's personal choice for the role. When other newspapers picked it up, the author issued a public retraction, apologizing to the star for any misunderstanding that might have arisen, and repeating, "I have never expressed a preference and never will."

Another widely publicized candidate was Norma Shearer, with whom Selznick had discussions concerning the part. But her fans created an outcry at the thought of an actress renowned for her sweet and ladylike qualities playing a southern minx; Ed Sullivan joined the protest in his column. In the end, in spite of encouragement from an editorial in the *New York Times*, Shearer graciously withdrew from the race, and became another star whose career was deeply affected by not playing Scarlett. Long impatient with her refined image, Shearer now pressed MGM for the *femme fatale* part in *Idiot's Delight*, in which she played opposite Gable immediately before he started *Gone With the Wind*.

The list of actresses who wanted to play Scarlett, or were touted for it by the fan magazines, press and radio commentators, and their agents, is amazing not only for variety but incongruity. Remembering that the story begins with Scarlett at the age of sixteen, it seems extraordinary that among the serious contenders were Shearer (thirty-seven), Miriam Hopkins (thirty-five), Tallulah Bankhead (thirty-four), Joan Crawford, Jean Arthur and Irene Dunne (all thirty-three). Some of these were actually tested. This is a comment, of course, from a society that is much more conscious of age (or youth) than were the '30s. The most popular figures of that time were women rather than girls. In Jean Arthur's case, one suspects the test to have been partly a sentimental gesture, since Selznick was in love with her before he married Mayer's daughter. An original and charming actress, she was clearly too old for the part, with no hint of the southern belle in her temperament, and the test looks strained and embarrassing. So does Bankhead's, for mainly the same reasons; demureness was never her stock-in-trade. Miriam Hopkins, who read for the part but didn't make a test, came from the South and had recently starred in the movie of *Becky Sharp*; the similarities between Thackeray's and Margaret Mitchell's heroine had been pointed out in several reviews. She had a strange, powerful intensity and like Shearer could create the illusion of physical glamor. You feel she might have gotten away with Scarlett on the stage.

Other actresses tested were Joan Bennett (from *Little Women*), Paulette Goddard, the young Lana Turner, who had just attracted attention in her first, small movie role in *They Won't Forget*, and a New York model called Edythe Marriner whom Irene Selznick had spotted at a fashion show. Loretta Young was also a favorite possibility with Selznick for a while. To see the film on the contenders is to see why Cukor and Selznick continued to hold out. Some are instantly out of the question: Lana Turner at sea, dazed and ringleted. Edythe Marriner — who changed her name to Susan Hayward after the test — looks right; she was nineteen then, with a slight resemblance to Vivien Leigh, but there's already a career-girl toughness in her screen presence. Paulette Goddard, recently launched by Chaplin in *Modern Times*, is the only one who comes close. Chaplin had sensed her *gamine* quality and brought it out very effectively in his film; in the test it is still there, appealing but somehow too city-ish for the daughter of Tara. Still, for a while she was under the most serious consideration, and then almost signed. Selznick changed his mind, for reasons that will appear later.

Of all these, Hopkins was the most hotly tipped by the press; coincidentally she had also worked in Cukor's stock company. He admired her talent, but says he never felt she was right for Scarlett. Other names tossed into the arena were Carole Lombard, Margaret Sullavan (both represented by Myron), Claudette Colbert, Ann Sheridan and Jean Harlow, but here we seem to enter the land of delusion and publicity gimmicks. And when Selznick asked the other studios to suggest any actresses they might have under contract, RKO came up with a twenty-seven-year-old unknown called Lucille Ball. "Are you kidding?" was her forthright reaction, but the casting agent pressed a vocal coach on her and arranged a reading with Selznick. He was polite but noncommittal. (A few years later she was sent for an equally unsuitable audition to Orson Welles, for the part of the girl whom *Citizen Kane* tries to turn into an opera singer.)

Publicity made it appear that Selznick spent most of his time from the end of 1936 to the fall of 1938 supervising the search for Scarlett, auditioning and looking at tests. In fact, he was busier in other directions: the search for a script was to prove equally exhaustive. He first engaged the Broadway playwright, Sidney Howard (*They Knew What They Wanted, The Silver Cord, Dodsworth*) to write a basic draft. The winner of a Pulitzer Prize, Howard had all the prestige credentials and some familiarity with movie technique, since he had previously worked with Goldwyn. Selznick's only doubt — which was to prove justified — was whether the distinguished easterner would be amenable to the producer's exacting methods of work. "I have never had much success with leaving a writer alone to do a script without almost daily collaboration with myself and usually also the director," he wrote in a cabled memo to Kay Brown, who was negotiating Howard's deal in New York. "Anything you can do to make Howard available for conference with us during the actual writing of the script will, I think, be safeguard." However, like many New York playwrights, Howard was not fundamentally interested in writing for films, and didn't care for California. He agreed only to come out to Hollywood for meetings with Selznick and Cukor, then went back East to work. He wrote to Margaret Mitchell, expressing delight with his assignment and asking for help on the Negro dialogue. Once again she refused to become involved. Howard embarked on what he considered a well-paid craftsman's job, and performed it with skill and considerable speed, structuring a series of master scenes from the half-million words of the novel in two months. While basically sound, clearing away many repetitions and disposable minor characters, it still presented a problem: it was over four hundred pages long, almost six hours' running time on the screen.

Selznick's first reaction was to consider making the film as two pictures. Faced with his principle of adhering faithfully to a classic, he was alarmed that further cuts might betray it. He had been thinking in terms of a picture that would run about two and a half hours, but Howard's first draft, even with all its omissions from the book, made it clear that *Gone With the Wind* could never be contained within this length. The idea of two separate pictures was dropped when Selznick learned that theater owners reacted unfavorably to it; instead, he asked Howard to come back to California and discuss with Cukor and himself more drastic ways of cutting the material down to size. At these talks, several new and deep incisions were made. They agreed to exclude from the film all members of the O'Hara family not living at Tara; Selznick wanted to "lose" Scarlett's second marriage, to Frank Kennedy, but both Cukor and Howard were against this, so they dropped only the child of that marriage; also, at Cukor's insistence, Scarlett's child by her first marriage was axed; all the Ku Klux Klan episodes were thrown out; and Howard was reproached for having added some scenes showing Rhett as a blockade runner. In this way the script was cut by another seventy pages or so, and Howard went home again.

Selznick then laid the script, such as it was, aside. Sporadically over the next few months he checked all the favorite scenes and lines that he'd noted in his own copy of the novel, to see if Howard's structure allowed for them; but he made no move to engage

Howard or anyone else to proceed with further writing. When Cukor inquired about this, Selznick's reply was somewhat evasive: "I am weighing every line and every word most carefully. . . . We are also double checking against our Story Department's notes on things that they missed from the book." Struck by Howard's comment at their last meeting that Margaret Mitchell "did everything at least twice," he ordered an assistant to make a complete index of the book, listing the main characters and what happened to them, how many times Rhett talked about the War and Ashley about the dissolution of the South, and so on, with the idea of eliminating repetitions and choosing the best passages of dialogue to combine from related scenes.

So by the end of January 1938, Howard's original draft was effectively on the shelf, along with piles of suggested cuts and revisions. Part of the reason for this was that, although Selznick was on the whole pleased with Howard's progress so far, he was displeased by the writer's refusal to stay out in California indefinitely and continue to work under his supervision. Already, in the back of his mind, Selznick was casting about for a more amenable successor; but in the front of his mind were several pictures he'd committed to produce, and he had no intention of relaxing his detailed personal control over any of them.

While Howard was still working on the script, *The Prisoner of Zenda* finished shooting, and Selznick decided it needed a number of retakes as well as a new director to stage the fencing scenes between Rudolf Rassendyll and Rupert of Hentzau. *A Star is Born* was also nearly finished, after five writers had worked on the script. In addition, Selznick was preparing a comedy, *Nothing Sacred*, a romantic drama, *Made For Each Other*, and another literary classic, *The Adventures of Tom Sawyer*. On this last, in a prophecy of things to come, the director, H. C. Potter (new to Hollywood from the theater), found Selznick's interference during shooting unbearable, and was replaced by Norman Taurog.

With so much simultaneous activity—the other films to produce, the mounds of notes accumulating on what was only a skeleton script of *Gone With the Wind*, the talent search, the testing of actresses, the negotiations with Gable and MGM — it is remarkable how Selznick, as Cukor said later, "kept the whole thing in his head and stuck with it." In fact, the whole thing was never really in anyone else's head. Justifying his methods of total control, Selznick declared that a film, in order to be a work of art, had to bear a personal signature, like a painting. In this way he expounded the *auteur* theory years ahead of his time, with the difference that to him the *auteur* was the producer and not the director.

The casting of Melanie and Ashley was only slightly less problematical. Anne Shirley, who suffered sweetly in *Anne of Green Gables* and *Stella Dallas*, Andrea Leeds, who attracted attention as the suicidal young actress in *Stage Door*, and Elizabeth Allan, the gentle mother of *David Copperfield*, were tested first. None quite hit the mark. Geraldine Fitzgerald and Priscilla Lane were considered, then dismissed. Selznick then approached Janet Gaynor, but the actress had decided to give up her screen career. One day Joan Fontaine, only twenty years old and under contract to RKO, where she'd had little success, came to see Cukor under the impression that he wanted her to read for Scarlett. When she found he was considering her for Melanie, she told him the part didn't interest her, but suggested it might interest her more famous sister, Olivia de Havilland. The idea interested Selznick and Cukor as well, and she came to the producer's home for a reading. De Havilland has described the experience: "George read Scarlett's lines while I read Melanie's. For some reason, George had to stand clutching some velvet curtains. He was absolutely marvelous — I'm sure it was his performance that got me the part." Both Selznick and Cukor agreed that she was the Melanie they wanted, but Warners' had to be approached again, since the actress was under contract there. At first Jack Warner refused a loan-out on any terms; like others in the industry he felt that *Gone With the Wind* was a foolhardy project and predicted, "It's going to be the biggest bust of all time."

In spite of the demure parts in which she'd been cast so far, nice virginal girls in love with the dashing Errol Flynn, de Havilland was spirited and shrewd. She went to work on Warner's wife, knowing her influence, and played a very effective tea-and-sympathy scene with her one afternoon at the Brown Derby. Mrs. Warner's influence was brought to bear on her husband, negotiations were opened, and a deal signed.

For Ashley, Selznick's first choice had always been Leslie Howard, then at the peak of his reputation as a "sensitive" leading man in movies and the theater. After *The Petrified Forest* and *Of Human Bondage*, he played *Hamlet* on the New York stage, then went back to England to give his best performance in the film of *Pygmalion*. Never really comfortable in his profession, mistrustful of "stardom" and the romantic image, Howard at this time was writing a play (which he never finished), and wanted to produce and direct. Approached by Selznick on his return to Hollywood, the actor's response was lukewarm. He was not interested in reading Margaret Mitchell's novel, and in fact never did so; when Selznick showed him a few scenes from the script, he remained unimpressed. Irene suggested Ray Milland, who interested her husband for a while; he tested Melvyn Douglas with Lana Turner, and while he thought Douglas gave "the first intelligent reading we've had," he felt him physically and temperamentally wrong for the part. Robert Young and Lew Ayres were briefly in the running, then definitely out of it. Discouraged, Selznick reproached himself for not having launched another talent search to discover an unknown Ashley. All the known possibilities, now including Leslie Howard — whose continued lack of response made Selznick doubt his original choice — suddenly seemed stale. "All we have to do is line up a complete cast of such people as Hepburn and Leslie Howard," a memo caustically observed, "and we can have a lovely picture for release eight years ago." Nevertheless he went back to Howard. Knowing the actor's other ambitions, he offered him a package deal, with a job to follow as associate producer on a forthcoming picture. Howard finally took the bait, giving the usual reason in a letter to his daughter in England: "Money is the mission here and who am I to refuse it?"

The forthcoming picture was to be *Intermezzo*. During the fall of 1938 Selznick also found time to follow up another tip from Kay Brown, who had seen Ingrid Bergman in the Swedish version, and to sign the actress to a contract. His schedule, it seemed, could never be full enough, and he embarked on plans for an American remake.

By November 1938, ten months after the final meetings with Sidney Howard, there had still been no progress on the script, and there was still no Scarlett; but a date had been fixed for the start of shooting. The deal with MGM specified that Gable had to begin work during the second week of February 1939, and there was no guarantee that he would be available for more than twenty weeks, which was less than the established shooting schedule. (In case it is wondered how a schedule could be established without a script, Selznick had given his production department a list of all the principal scenes and sets that would definitely be included in the picture, and on this basis the department worked out a shooting period of approximately twenty-two weeks. Simultaneously, the many background and incidental shots not requiring direction of actors would be done by second units.) Now pressed for time, Selznick announced that a single sequence, the burning of Atlanta, would be shot on December 10, 1938. He planned to use the following two months, until Gable was available, on further preparation and on scenes without Rhett.

During November, too, he almost found his Scarlett. Reviewing all the known and unknown actresses tested or considered so far, he decided to narrow down the final list to Hepburn, Joan Bennett, Jean Arthur and Loretta Young, having apparently forgotten in some cases his recent warning to himself about producing a picture for release eight years ago. As usual, second thoughts occurred, and he asked Cukor to make another test of Paulette Goddard. He viewed the result several times, and found himself increasingly impressed. Third thoughts occurred. Cukor had also tested an unknown actress called Dorothy Jordan, the wife of Merian C. Cooper. Selznick now ordered another test of her, also viewed it several times; while he found it promising, it never quite caught fire. Finally he came to a decision. Paulette Goddard would be his Scarlett O'Hara, and her agent was contacted. However, at this time Chaplin and his star were publicly living together, and no one was certain whether or not they were married. In more paranoid circles of the movie industry and the middle classes, Chaplin's alleged left-wing views in *Modern Times* had caused the first stirrings of the unpopularity that was to drive him out of the country ten years later. Now the cry of an "immoral" private life was raised. When it became known that Goddard was on the verge of being signed, women's clubs all over the United States fired salvos of protest. Such things were far more serious then than now, and Selznick felt obliged to ask his Scarlett whether she was Chaplin's wife. Goddard insisted that a ceremony had occurred at sea, in the harbor of Singapore, while they were on a cruise to the Orient. (In *My Autobiography*, published in 1964, Chaplin states briefly, "During this trip Paulette and I were married.") Unfortunately Goddard couldn't produce a marriage certificate, or any official evidence that the wedding had taken place. Deciding not to risk a scandal, Selznick reluctantly ordered the search to continue.*

In the meantime he turned his attention again briefly to the script. After Margaret Mitchell refused his offer to inspect the existing material and give her opinion of it, he engaged Oliver H. P. Garrett, a screenwriter with whom he'd previously worked at MGM, to collaborate with him on further revisions to the structure and continuity. This job began on the train to New York, where Selznick had to go for a week of business meetings. Together he and Garrett made some more cuts and reworked several major scenes — the barbecue at Twelve Oaks, the meeting of Rhett and Scarlett at the Atlanta Bazaar, the escape from Atlanta, Ashley's return from the War, and the new events leading up to the death of Frank Kennedy. Like other writers who came after him, Garrett was limited in several ways: by being allowed to work only on isolated sequences, by the fact that Selznick was still uncertain how long a film he wanted, and by the warnings not to tamper with a classic. "The ideal script, as far as I am concerned, would be one that did not contain a single word of original dialogue, and that was one hundred per cent Margaret Mitchell, however much we juxtaposed it." A difficult order when Selznick also demanded the invention of an occasional scene not in the book.

Like his successors, Garrett was employed only for a week or two, and never knew which of his ideas had been accepted until he saw the finished picture. Until the middle of January 1939, other writers — including John van Druten, Scott Fitzgerald

* The Chaplin–Goddard marriage — or the date of it, at least — remains a mystery. At the premiere of *The Great Dictator* in 1940, Chaplin introduced her to journalists as his wife, but shortly afterwards she left for Mexico and returned with a divorce. It was widely speculated that, having already decided to separate, they had in fact married only a few months earlier, in order to go through the formality of a divorce. Whatever really happened, the situation cost Paulette Goddard the legendary role.

and the scenarist Jo Swerling — were brought in to work in the same piecemeal way. In spite of his demands for close collaboration, Selznick never seems to have been willing to work with his writers for more than a few days (or nights) at a time, and to have remained curiously indifferent to the confusion his methods created. As late as a day before the start of principal photography, a note to Whitney tells him not to worry about "the seemingly small amount of final revised script. . . . It is so clearly in my mind that I can tell you the picture from beginning to end, almost shot for shot."

While the mounds of unrevised pages continued to grow, he began conferring with Cukor on the casting of supporting parts. Lionel Barrymore was their first idea for Dr. Meade, but the actor was by now confined to a wheelchair, and they chose Harry Davenport instead. Selznick asked Kay Brown to sound out Tallulah Bankhead (now officially rejected as a candidate for Scarlett) whether she would play Belle Watling, the Atlanta madam; Bankhead's reply, though not recorded, can be imagined, and the role went to Ona Munson. Hattie McDaniel was tested and cast as Mammy, Thomas Mitchell signed for Scarlett's father and Barbara O'Neil (after Lillian Gish turned the part down) for her mother. Laura Hope Crews, a specialist in silly old women, landed Aunt Pittypat after Billie Burke was rejected as silly but not old enough.

The production team was already at work. For his designer Selznick chose William Cameron Menzies, with whom he'd already been associated on *Tom Sawyer*, and who had other notable achievements to his credit, from the silent *Thief of Bagdad* with Fairbanks to *Things to Come* in England, which he also co-directed. According to Cukor, Hobe Erwin (who made the charming sets for *Little Women*) was also importantly involved in early conferences on the visual aspects, and influenced the general approach. Since both Menzies and Erwin are dead, this is one of several production matters that cannot be totally cleared up. Erwin has no credit on the film, and only worked on it for a few weeks before being replaced as art director by Lyle Wheeler; but this in itself is no reason to doubt Cukor's claim that he contributed vital ideas. On the other hand, there is the evidence of Menzies' involvement with the film throughout; his direction of several sequences; the color sketches for all the major camera set-ups in every scene that his assistant, Macmillan Johnson, made under his supervision; the sets he designed that were executed by Lyle Wheeler. And further evidence exists in the very individual talent that can be found in Menzies' previous and subsequent work.

The range of color in *Tom Sawyer*, the stunning city of the future in *Things to Come*, the atmospheric sets for *Kings Row*, *Ivy*, and Hitchcock's *Foreign Correspondent* — all these show the touch of a master. But Menzies was one of those talents whose lack of specialization makes him difficult to sum up. He designed films, occasionally directed them, sometimes only executed other people's designs, but in every case visualized the whole look of a production, lighting and camera angles as well as the sets themselves. The "line" in his work is a purely physical one, and on this basis alone it is difficult to think of another artist who could have combined such extremes of monumental effect and fine detail for *Gone With the Wind*.

Lee Garmes, the cameraman assigned to the picture, had done brilliant innovative work throughout the '30s; he was a pioneer in the development of low-key lighting, rich and muted halftones, seen at their most spectacular in the von Sternberg–Dietrich films, *Morocco*, *Shanghai Express* and *Dishonored*. A cable from Selznick reached him in London, where he'd been working for several months with Alexander Korda on a project now in a state of collapse — *Cyrano de Bergerac*, to star Charles Laughton. By coincidence, Garmes (who was going to direct it) had just tested Vivien Leigh for Roxanne. Disagreements between Korda and Laughton caused the film to be abandoned. Garmes remembers that Selznick's cable astonished him, since he was convinced — from all the publicity that had reached him at a distance — that *Gone With the Wind* must at least have started shooting. After his agent checked that it was not so, Garmes returned to Hollywood a day too late to film the burning of Atlanta, with which production began. He then worked on the picture for seven weeks, after which he had differences of opinion with Selznick and was replaced. Although he shot almost a third of the picture, and Vivien Leigh's tests, he received no credit.

For the costumes Selznick turned to Walter Plunkett, with whom he'd already worked on *Little Women*, and who had the eerie task of creating petticoats and crinolines for a nonexistent Scarlett. For the interiors, Joseph B. Platt, head of a large designing firm, was brought out from New York. He created special wallpapers and carpets, and supervised the choice of antique furniture. Both he and Plunkett worked in close collaboration with Menzies, evolving color effects and motifs for different scenes. Naturally Selznick attended all their conferences and gave his seal of approval to the sketches.

Tara was to be built on the studio back lot, where various sets from *The Last of the Mohicans*, *King Kong*, *The Garden of Allah*, and *Little Lord Fauntleroy* were still standing. Selznick's production manager, Raymond Klune, suggested that instead of clearing them away, they should be reassembled, repainted, and then burned as Atlanta. Since this was to be a night scene, and much of the detail would be obscured by raging flames, it took only a few false fronts to prepare them for destruction.

While the old sets were being readied for burning, Selznick had a further brief attack of interest in the script. With another Russian friend, Jo Swerling, who had written the screenplay of the studio's recently completed *Made For Each Other*, he went

to Bermuda for a week. Notes were taken, but no writing accomplished. Returning to Hollywood, he was momentarily alarmed by Eddie Mannix, a vice-president of MGM, who told him that the burning of Atlanta could be carried out much more effectively by the use of model shots. Menzies and Raymond Klune emphatically disagreed, and after some hesitation, Selznick allowed the plan to proceed.

The night of the 10th, the night of the fire, was cold. Seven Technicolor cameras — all that were available in Hollywood at that time — had been positioned to cover the burning, of which there could obviously be no retakes, and the set-ups and lighting were worked out by Ray Rennahan, the cameraman-adviser supplied by Technicolor.* Pipes had been run through the old sets, carrying gasoline which would ignite them, twenty-five members of the Los Angeles police department, fifty studio firemen and two hundred studio helpers were standing by with equipment and 5,000-gallon water tanks in case the flames should get out of hand. Sets of doubles were engaged for Scarlett and Rhett, who would be seen in various long and medium shots as they escaped from the city with Melanie, her newborn baby, and Prissy the maid hidden in the back of the wagon. A special look-out platform had been built for Selznick, his mother (Lewis J. Selznick had moved to California in the early thirties and died soon afterwards) and friends. Myron was expected, but had warned he might be late since he was entertaining some clients at dinner.

* The first feature film to be shot entirely in "three-strip" Technicolor, *Becky Sharp*, had been made only four years previously. This relatively new process involved exposure of three separate strips of negative simultaneously, and, while the equipment was cumbersome, it allowed a far greater range and control than the earlier "two-strip" method. It had, in fact, been considerably improved since its earlier use. The Technicolor company supplied a special cameraman and assistant to act as technical advisers on each production, checking the amount of light and the kinds of filters used. This explains the credit of Rennahan and Wilfrid Cline on *Gone With the Wind*. One-strip or monopack Technicolor, which greatly facilitated its general use, was not perfected until several years later.

There was something Napoleonic in the image of the thirty-seven-year-old producer elevated on his platform, surrounded by a court, waiting to give the order that would set the world on fire. However, since Myron was late, the order was delayed — like almost everything else connected with the picture. After an hour, Ray Klune told Selznick that it was impossible to keep the police and fire departments waiting any longer. Intensely nervous — what if Mannix should prove right, and the highly publicized funeral pyre fail to make its impact on the screen? — the producer gave his signal. Instantly the famous old sets, their wood dried for months in the California summer, began to blaze. Cukor called the first "Action!" on *Gone With the Wind*, and the doubles of Scarlett and Rhett made their escape past the burning structures of *King Kong* and *The Garden of Allah*.

As the sparks flew upward and the buildings began to tremble, Selznick knew that Mannix had been wrong. He turned to Raymond Klune and apologized for having doubted him. Blazing fragments soared into the darkness, and Lee Zavitz, in charge of special effects for the sequence, remembers the firemen shooting them down with their hoses, "like ducks." And to some Los Angeles residents, always fearful of natural disasters such as earthquakes and holocausts, the overpowering glow in the sky announced that the city itself was on fire. A few dozen people hastily packed suitcases, got into their cars and started driving toward the desert.

As the fire began to wane and the shooting ended, Myron arrived, slightly drunk, with his dinner guests. He led them up to the platform, ignoring David's reproaches and excitedly seizing his arm. "I want you to meet your Scarlett O'Hara!" he said loudly, causing everybody to turn around.

Selznick looked from the acres of burning rubble to a young actress standing beside Laurence Olivier. Firelight seemed to accentuate the hint of pale green in the light blue of her eyes, the green that Margaret Mitchell had ascribed to the eyes of her heroine. He knew that she was Vivien Leigh, an English actress, and that she and Olivier were in love. He also knew that several months ago her name had been mentioned to him by one of his talent executives, and he'd screened two pictures she made in Britain, *Fire Over England* and *A Yank at Oxford*, thought her excellent but in no way a possible Scarlett. Seeing her now, the moment turned into a scene from his own *A Star is Born*. "I took one look and knew that she was right — at least right as far as her appearance went," he said later. "If you have a picture of someone in mind and then suddenly you see that person, no more evidence is necessary. . . . I'll never recover from that first look."

four

SCARLETT

TOWARD THE END OF HER LIFE, Vivien Leigh turned against Scarlett. "I never liked Scarlett. I knew it was a marvelous part, but I never cared for her." She also insisted that she had never gone after the role, that she believed Cukor still favored Katharine Hepburn, and that the test was only a "lark." By this time, no doubt, she was tired of being haunted by a legend; and she was not well, and not happy. The truth is that she read the book in London when it first came out, and was eager for the role. With an intuition and courage that were typical of her, she even thought she would get it. She once admitted this to me herself — "Yes, of course I wanted it" — and in 1960, in an interview with David Lewin for the London *Daily Express*, she publicly confirmed it: "Everyone said I was mad to try for *Gone With the Wind*, but I wanted it and I knew I'd get it. The only thing I didn't want was the seven-year film contract that went with it."

When she went to Hollywood early in December 1938 it was on a sudden impulse, very Scarlett-like in its mixture of romance and ambition. Laurence Olivier and she were in love, although both were still married to others — Vivien to Dr. Leigh Holman and Olivier to the actress Jill Esmond (who'd tested for Hepburn's part in *A Bill of Divorcement*). Vivien was about to start rehearsals for her role of Titania in a production of *A Midsummer Night's Dream* at the Old Vic, while Olivier had already gone out to California for the filming of *Wuthering Heights*. Both thought of themselves as primarily theater people and were suspicious of Hollywood. Olivier had a personal grudge against the place, having gone there in 1933 to test for the lead opposite Garbo in *Queen Christina* and lost out to John Gilbert. He returned to England and soon became a major star in the theater. When William Wyler, who was going to direct *Wuthering Heights* for Goldwyn, came to London to offer Olivier the part of Heathcliff, the actor at first refused. He didn't want to go back to Hollywood. Then he said he might do it if Vivien could play Cathy; but Merle Oberon had already been cast. Partly as a bribe, but partly because he had gone to a preview of Vivien's latest film, *Sidewalks of London*, and had been impressed by her, Wyler offered her the role of Isabella Linton. Vivien turned it down, wanting Cathy or nothing. "For a first part in Hollywood, you'll get nothing better than this," the director warned her, but she refused to heed him, and Isabella went to Geraldine Fitzgerald.

In spite of his doubts, and the separation from Vivien that would result, Olivier found the prospect of Heathcliff irresistible after all. But he was soon writing unhappy letters to Vivien — he had athlete's foot and was hobbling around on crutches; the film was going very badly; he felt he was not getting any help from Wyler, who gave all his attention to Merle Oberon; and this was naturally affecting his relationship with his leading lady. He implied that she might even walk off the picture. So Vivien went to Hollywood because he was unhappy, and because there seemed a chance that she might play Cathy after all. She was supposed to return within two weeks to start work at the Old Vic, but it was almost two years before she went back to England.

The chance of replacing Merle Oberon did not in fact exist. There were problems at first on *Wuthering Heights*, but if anyone was in danger of losing a part, it was Olivier. Merle Oberon has described to me how, after two weeks of shooting, Sam Goldwyn came on the set and told Wyler and Olivier that he was not satisfied with the actor's performance. He found it too theatrical, and thought Olivier was using an unnecessarily squalid and repulsive make-up for the Heathcliff of the early sequences. As a result, the scenes were reshot and Wyler began devoting most of his attention to Olivier. In spite of the false start and all the tensions, the actor found his way to an extraordinary performance that made him an international movie star.

No Cathy, then; but Scarlett O'Hara was still not cast, and Myron Selznick was Olivier's agent. Vivien had told Olivier how much she wanted the part, and he asked Myron to introduce her to David. At first Myron was tentative, then at the burning of Atlanta the moment suddenly arranged itself. When they met on the platform, Selznick was so electrified by the look of Vivien that he asked her almost at once if she'd like to make a test. She was clever enough to express surprise, then agreed.

Next day Selznick took her to Cukor's office. The director also knew little about her at the time. Although Vivien had become a star on the London stage in *The Mask of Virtue* and had made several films for Korda, British movies in those days had little distribution in the United States; only *A Yank at Oxford*, made by MGM, meant anything at all there. But Cukor liked the look of her too, and with his acute nose for talent felt something "exciting" in her presence. He asked her to read one of the test scenes and was immediately disconcerted by her English accent. "She began reading this thing very sweetly, and very, very clipped. . . . So I struck her across the face with the rudest thing I could say. She screamed with laughter. That was the beginning of our most tender, wonderful friendship." He arranged to shoot a test next day.

In the actress who should play Scarlett, Cukor has said, he was always looking for someone "charged with electricity" and who seemed "possessed of the devil." It is certain that Vivien Leigh was in some way possessed. The exterior was all beauty, grace, manners, charm; beneath it was something neurotic and driven that perhaps she herself never really understood. There was a duality in her nature, as marked as the break in the body of a rock. In a cool, precisely offhand voice she could throw off alarming confidences such as, "I've never slept much, ever. Since I was born, I haven't slept much." There would be no hint of it in her appearance. Although she once said, "I could never find anything of Scarlett in myself," this side of her temperament, the mixture of exquisite control and passionate excess, was very close to the way Margaret Mitchell described her heroine: "The green eyes in the carefully sweet face were turbulent, willful, lusty with life, distinctly at variance with her decorous demeanor." It seems impossible that an actress should have passionately wanted a part with which she felt she couldn't make personal contact. Although the scheming, shallowly flirtatious aspect of Scarlett was alien to her, I think she responded very much to something driven and desperate in the character.

Cukor had tested another actress before Vivien that day, and Vivien always remembered that when she got into Scarlett's costume it was still warm. The test was in black-and-white, and she played two scenes, with Hattie McDaniel as Mammy lacing up her corset for the Wilkes barbecue, and with Leslie Howard as Ashley, when she first declares her love for him during a siesta at the barbecue. A few days later she made a third test —

Just before the technicolor cameras roll, Vivien Leigh gives her lines a last once-over. To her left is Susan Myrick, "The Emily Post of Dixie," engaged to advise on dialect and manners.

coached in the meantime for a southern accent by Susan Myrick, known as the "Emily Post of the South," one of several experts engaged to advise on dialect and manners. This was a later scene with Ashley, soon after the War has ended; Scarlett makes another, even more passionate declaration of love and suggests that they run away together.

To see these tests is to witness one of those instantaneous understandings between actress and part. The southern accent

Scarlett is signed early January 1939: Cukor, Vivien Leigh,
Selznick, Olivia de Havilland, Leslie Howard.

hardly exists in the first two, but it doesn't matter. In every other
way Vivien Leigh *becomes* Scarlett, and the boldness and confidence of an actress only twenty-five years old, required to show
her grasp of a role with hardly any preparation at all, is extraordinary. In contrast to the others who tested, what is unique and
immediately striking is her passion. "There was an indescribable
wildness about her," Cukor remembered later. She is never coy
or tentative or strained, and instead of playing the first scene with
Ashley like a schoolgirl with a crush, she is direct in her desire

for him, dangerously impatient. The third test is the most highly charged of all. Within a few days she has basically mastered the southern accent, which slips away only now and then, and since Howard was not available that day is playing with another Ashley, but the woodenness of Douglass Montgomery in no way deters her. Now she presents a woman instead of a girl, hardened by experience, with an underlying panic and desperation; the scene becomes a fierce, disturbing appeal to Ashley to save her life. In fact the performance here is more striking than when she repeats it in the film under Victor Fleming's direction.

Five days went by after the last test, and she heard nothing. Strangely confident, she cabled Tyrone Guthrie in London, explaining the situation and asking for her release from A Midsummer Night's Dream, which was granted. Selznick's hesitation after seeing the tests might appear incredible, but the delay had nothing to do with her performance. Both he and Cukor were convinced they had found their Scarlett. However, Selznick was worried both by the fact that she was English and, remembering the problem with Paulette Goddard, having a love affair with Olivier while both of them were still married to other people. How much public hostility would be created by the announcement that an English actress had been chosen to play Scarlett? "The idea of it seemed outrageous," Cukor remembers. Though two of the other leading players were English, presumably Leslie Howard and Olivia de Havilland were thought of as American because of having worked in Hollywood for several years. The public's disapproval was far less than feared; and a threat by the Florida branch of the United Daughters of the Confederacy to boycott the film seemed a small price to pay. On the second score, both Olivier and Vivien assured Selznick that they were filing suits for divorce and intended to get married.

On Christmas Day 1938, Cukor gave a lunch party at his house. Vivien and Olivier were among the guests. Soon after they arrived, Cukor took Vivien aside and told her the part had been cast. She supposed he meant Hepburn was to play it after all. He shook his head and told her, "I guess we're stuck with you."

There remained a final deal to be made. Selznick bought Vivien's contract from Korda, who told her she was making a foolish mistake: "You are completely wrong for the part. . . ." For the longest leading role in what was to become the longest and most profitable movie ever made in Hollywood, she was paid $30,000 and would remain under contract to Selznick until 1945. Her mixed reactions, and evidence that Cukor was the deciding factor, are provided in the first of several letters she wrote to her husband, with whom she remained on friendly terms:

"As you so well realize, I loathe Hollywood and for no other part would I have dreamt of signing a contract. . . . All their standards are financial ones, and I am doing *Gone With the Wind* for them for less money than I have been earning, per picture, for the last two years. The director of the picture was in the theatre for a long time and is a very intelligent and imaginative man and seems to understand the subject perfectly." (January 25, 1939) five

INSIDE
THE WHALE

F ROM THE ASHES of Atlanta, under a winter sky, arose the set of Tara, carefully romanticized from Margaret Mitchell's description. A graveled driveway, lined with arching cedars, led past a wide green lawn to the plantation house of whitewashed brick. Trucks arrived with loads of brick dust, mixed into the surrounding earth to make it look southern red. "From the avenue of cedars to the row of white cabins in the slave quarters," the author had written, "there was an air of solidness, of stability and permanence about Tara." There was also an air of opulence about its reproduction which, when Selznick sent her photographs of it, she privately found exaggerated. She commented to a friend that she'd always thought of Tara as "upcountry functional," and that she would like to found a society called "The Association of Southerners Whose Grandpappies Did Not Live in Houses with White Columns." (Later, when Selznick sent her photographs of the designs for Twelve Oaks, the Wilkes house, she told the same friend, "I rolled on the floor screaming with laughter.") As for Tara's white columns, Susan Myrick proved her worth early on by pointing out to Selznick that at least they should not be rounded; and the design was corrected to make them squared, in the authentic style of the Old South rather than of the studio facade. Shortly afterwards, she made another objection; Selznick planned to insert a descriptive scene of cotton being chopped on the O'Hara plantation, immediately before the Twelve Oaks barbecue. However, news of Lincoln's declaration of war arrived during the barbecue and established the date as mid-April. "Planting time," Miss Myrick said. "He just couldn't chop cotton then." In his curious obsessive way, the producer argued with her through a score of memos, from February until late May. "He had hired the Hall Johnson Choir to sing as they chopped, and he HAD to go ahead with the scene." Finally he gave up.

There was no question of any serious location work in the South, although the famous maker of travelogues, James Fitzpatrick, was commissioned to make a few background shots. (None of them was finally used, except for the shot of the Mississippi riverboat on which Rhett and Scarlett start their honeymoon.) The tradition of Hollywood film-making in the thirties was that you could make everything look better by building a set, and the kind of vast, nostalgic, quintessential evocation of the South that Selznick wanted could only be achieved at the studio. For the fields surrounding Tara, locations were chosen in the San Fernando Valley, its earth again tinted red, and the gardens of a private estate in Pasadena.

At the same time, construction was under way on the sound stages of the interiors of Tara, Lyle Wheeler executing Menzies' designs for the sets and Joseph Platt contacting dealers across the country for hundreds of pieces of authentic furniture. Selznick was particularly concerned with the "reality" of these, stressing the importance of aging them, to avoid the usual look of sets and props that had just arrived the night before. Wilbur G. Kurtz, an artist and historian of the South, was retained to check on every detail, and various assistants were employed to verify such things as how horses' tails were cropped at the time and whether oral thermometers were used in hospitals. All the stars were summoned for extensive costume and make-up tests, and another specialist in southern dialect, Will A. Price, joined Susan Myrick to coach them in accents. On another stage, the building of the set for the Atlanta Bazaar was under way. Menzies was also preparing a second huge exterior set, the city of Atlanta, with more than fifty buildings and a total of two miles of streets.

Surrounded by specialists of every kind and the largest army of studio workers ever assembled for a single movie, Selznick seemed to have only one major problem left: the script. It was still an unresolved mound, pink, yellow, and blue pages indicating rewrites of the original white, but less than a third of the scenes fully worked out and ready to shoot. For a few days John Van Druten, already at work rewriting *Intermezzo*, was called in to work on separate scenes; he was followed by Scott Fitzgerald for a few weeks. Instructed like the others to use only Margaret Mitchell's dialogue, Fitzgerald seems to have been the first to caution Selznick that there was already too much of it. He reminded him that in movies "it's dull and false for one character to describe another," and recommended that long speeches — such as Ashley's account to Scarlett of the desperate state of the Confederate army — should be reduced to a minimum, because the audience had already been shown what he was talking about. Fitzgerald would indicate, too, how an image or the expression on an actor's face could frequently replace dialogue. One scene he was given to rework was the moment when Scarlett watches Melanie and Ashley, recently married, go upstairs to bed. By this time the audience knew that Scarlett was still obsessed with Ashley and jealous of Melanie, but the previous version of the scene again reminded them of it in dialogue.

Fitzgerald's "rewrite" was a cutting of most of the lines, explaining in a note to Selznick: "It seems to me stronger in silence." Fitzgerald also discovered, rather to his surprise, that Margaret Mitchell's original dialogue was usually better than other writers' reworking of it. Again, there was often too much of it, but vital lines could be extracted to make the point better than any rephrasing. In a letter to his daughter he gave one of the fairest, most relevant estimates of the book as a whole: "not very original, in fact leaning heavily on *The Old Wives' Tale, Vanity Fair,* and all that has been written on the Civil War. . . . But on the other hand it is interesting, surprisingly honest, consistent and workmanlike throughout, and I felt no contempt for it, but only a certain pity for those who consider it the supreme achievement of the human mind."

With Sidney Howard having already pointed out to him the repetitions in the structure, and Fitzgerald now criticizing the dialogue for the same reason, Selznick actually held the key for a reexamination of his troubled script. He did not see it himself that way, however, and used hardly any of Fitzgerald's suggestions. Then, disappointed by the writer's failure to come up with some "funny" lines for Aunt Pittypat, he fired him. Being taken off the script was a disastrous blow to Fitzgerald's already shakey confidence. He began the long on-again-off-again drinking bout that led to his final decline and death eighteen months later. Another letter to his daughter, shortly after Selznick fired him, is an ironic valedictory to his unrequited love affair with the movies: "So farewell, Miriam Hopkins, who leans *so* close when she talks, so long, Claudette Colbert, as yet unencountered, mysterious Garbo, glamorous Dietrich, exotic Shirley Temple — you will never know me." However, between the drinking bouts and brief assignments on B pictures, he began *The Last Tycoon.* Although unfinished, it remains the most fascinating novel about Hollywood ever written, and sums up his feelings about the

Thalbergs and the Selznicks, those enigmatic, power-driven figures whom in spite of everything he wanted to please.

So Fitzgerald's pages joined the mass of others on the shelf, and Selznick showed little concern. He seemed infatuated with the physical creation of a world. Every other element came under painstaking supervision at this time, and he even sent an SOS to Margaret Mitchell, "How should we tie Mammy's bandana?" (Her answer: "I don't know, and I'm not going out on a limb over a headrag.") Meanwhile the basic material remained in a state of relative disorganization.

There were other reasons for this, beyond the mania for physical detail, wallpapers, fabrics for petticoats, bandanas. First, Selznick had begun to delude himself that he was a writer, a delusion that was to increase in later years. From the succession of writers after Sidney Howard,* he had gained a few satisfactory scenes and a few ideas, but he didn't leave them alone. In spite of all the other pressures, he found time to rewrite practically all the scenes himself. By now, of course, he regarded the film of *Gone With the Wind* as entirely his own conception, and perhaps it seemed logical to him that he could personally solve every problem. From time to time Cukor would complain about a scene not being ready, and Selznick's response was always the same: he would promise to work all night with one of the writers currently and momentarily on his payroll, and the scene would be perfect in the morning. Not surprisingly, the results failed to justify his promise.

For under the surface the strain was beginning to tell. In an article called "The Great Dictator," Alva Johnston has described Selznick's condition at this time. Not only would he work with-

---

* Other writers called in for a few days on the script, apart from those already mentioned, were John Balderston, who adapted *The Prisoner of Zenda*; the playwright Edwin Justus Mayer; and Charles MacArthur, the frequent collaborator of Ben Hecht. The results of their work, if any, remain unknown.

out sleeping for seventy-two hours at a stretch but, under his doctor's supervision, he had been put on "a daily ration of benzedrine and six or eight grains of thyroid extract — enough to send many a man to heaven. Rather than yield to fatigue, he occasionally left his office at two or three A.M. and went to a gambling house. This was an expensive cure for drowsiness, but after a few hours of roulette he would return to his office refreshed and wide awake, with all the fatigue toxins cleared out of his brain." Johnston also put forward the interesting theory that Selznick developed the habit of dictating memos because he hated to be interrupted while he was talking, and nobody can interrupt a memo. Selznick himself has said that he learned the habit from his father, who found dictation the best way of clarifying his thoughts. I think there was by now another reason. At a time when he was undertaking the most ambitious and strenuous work of his career, his expanding ego demanded a consciousness of posterity. He was documenting himself, and taking care that the documents should be preserved. In the same way, after the success of *Gone With the Wind* he ordered his publicity staff to write letters to the editors of all the major encyclopedias and reference books that did not yet include his name.

Pushing himself to the edge, propped up by drugs, sleeping irregularly, gambling compulsively, his marriage to Irene Mayer beginning to show signs of crisis (a tricky problem while he was in business with her father), Selznick's control was not as secure as it appeared to the world to be. These tensions account to a considerable extent for his failure to come to terms with the script, or with the other quarrels and emergencies that were to explode throughout much of the shooting.

On January 26, 1939, principal shooting began. The opening studio sequences — Scarlett on the porch at Tara, flirting with the Tarleton twins and complaining about their talk of war,

then getting ready for the Wilkes barbecue — were actually the first to be done. (The porch scene was reshot on Selznick's orders, because he wanted Scarlett to wear a white dress instead of the flowered muslin that she would also wear to the barbecue.) Then, because of the script situation, scenes were scheduled according to whether they already existed in practical form on paper, and which sets were ready. Cukor followed the opening with two other episodes taken very literally from the book, the birth of Melanie's child, with Scarlett forcing the hysterical Prissy (Butterfly McQueen) to help her deliver it, and the scene with the Union deserter who appears at Tara at the end of the

War and is shot by Scarlett. After this he completed the first scene with Gable, when Rhett brings Scarlett the present of a Paris hat. Then he moved to the set of the Atlanta Bazaar, and began the first day's shooting of the ball. At the end of it, when he'd been working on the picture for two and a half weeks, Selznick fired Cukor.

To this day Cukor says he is still uncertain of the reason. He had been Selznick's choice from the first; they had worked together for two years, between other films, making tests and conferring on the script, the design, and all the casting. At the time, it was widely believed that Gable had never wanted Cukor, that he was afraid of his reputation as a "women's director," and felt the picture would be thrown to Vivien Leigh. Cukor does not accept this. "If that's so, it was very naïve of him and not the thinking of a very good or professional actor. . . . I don't throw anything anywhere at all, there's the truth of the scene and it states itself." The one scene with Gable that he directed, which remains in the picture, certainly shows no favoritism toward Vivien Leigh; on the other hand, both Lee Garmes and Ray Klune have confirmed to me their impression that Gable — who was extremely nervous and tense throughout much of the shooting — was never happy with the choice of Cukor. Their only overt disagreement, in the brief time they worked together, was over the question of a southern accent, Cukar wanting the actor to attempt a more distinct one; but Selznick interfered, coming down on Gable's side.

Cukor has also said that for the first time in their relationship, even before shooting started, Selznick seemed to trust him less. "He wanted to attend the rehearsals, which I thought unwise. I was the director, after all, and a director should shoot the scene before the producer sees it. . . . And then David started coming down on the set, giving hot tips which weren't really very helpful. He'd never done that before. He changed our methods of working." In fact their relationship had changed in other ways since they first worked together. No longer the protégé, Cukor had become a highly successful director without Selznick by the time of *Gone With the Wind;* he had turned down *A Star Is Born,* not wanting to do another Hollywood movie so soon, preferring to direct *Camille* instead, and he had declined to replace H. C. Potter on *Tom Sawyer.* Selznick had not failed to comment privately, in a memo to one of his company associates, on the problems of "the Cukor situation."

Another clue is provided by Lee Garmes. In an interview with Charles Higham, he remarked, "It wasn't his fault that George was fired. It was David's. . . . All the preparatory work was based on Sidney Howard's script, but when we started shooting, we were using Selznick's. His own material didn't play the same. Cukor was too much of a gentleman to go to David and say, 'Look, you silly son-of-a-bitch, your writing isn't as good.'" Instead, Cukor directed some basically unplayable scenes to the best of his ability, "and no one else wanted to tell the Czar he was wrong." This point is borne out in another letter that Vivien Leigh wrote to her husband.

Pressure from MGM seems to have been another factor. First of all, if Gable were unhappy the studio would have wanted to placate him; and while it was clear from the start that the film would go some way over its original budget of $2,500,000, Cukor refused to sacrifice the nuances of detail and atmosphere so characteristic of his work. "Look at the scene where Mammy's lacing up Scarlett," Olivia de Havilland said later, "and then at the next one, where Scarlett sits on the stairs eating a chicken leg. There are no other scenes in the film with so much detail, such richness — all these were Cukor touches." Yet when Mayer saw the rushes, he expressed doubts. If Cukor paid so much attention to intimate moments, wouldn't he neglect the spectacle, the more commercial aspects of the story? It seems possible that

Mayer's reaction revived an ancient doubt in Selznick's mind. Originally he had thought of employing another director for the War sequences, and considered the idea of approaching D. W. Griffith; then, reluctantly, he decided that the old master was not up to it. Also, as Leslie Howard complained in a letter to his daughter, "after seven days' shooting they are five days behind schedule." Much of the delay, however, was caused by Selznick, who not only ordered the porch scene to be reshot but sent down his own revised scenes to the set almost every day.

Just as Cukor never really knew, neither perhaps did Selznick. From all that was happening — Gable's private complaints about Cukor, a shooting pace slower than he'd expected, and Cukor's evident resentment of his interferences — Selznick was bound to feel some unpromising vibrations and he knew that something had to be done. There is no evidence in any of Cukor's surviving work in the film that he was at fault, but it was almost impossible for him to escape taking the blame.

A joint statement issued to the press on February 13 began as follows: "As a result of a series of disagreements between us over many of the individual scenes of *Gone With the Wind*, we have mutually decided that the only solution is for a new director to be selected at as early a date as is practicable."

Costumed in black, Vivien Leigh and Olivia de Havilland were rehearsing a scene at the Atlanta Bazaar when the news was brought. They burst into tears and ran over to Selznick's office, where they pleaded with him for almost an hour to change his mind. They said that Cukor had done all the groundwork on their roles, that he had laid them out in detail; but Selznick remained unyielding.

In fact, although Cukor shot very little of the picture, his imprint remained even after his departure. De Havilland called him one day to ask if she could come over to his house for a few hours on Sundays (there was a six-day work week at the time) and, as Cukor puts it, "do some moonlighting." They would run scenes together. One day the actress asked Cukor if he thought she was wrong to be doing this behind Vivien's back. He told her that he couldn't see why, since Vivien was doing exactly the same thing. Until the end of shooting, in fact, Cukor "ghosted" their performances in this way.

Naturally production had to close down after Cukor's dismissal, and the episode seemed to confirm a general doubt in Hollywood about the entire project. "The whole town was against us," de Havilland remembers, "and there wasn't a soul in Hollywood who wished us well." Vivien wrote in another letter to her husband: "He [Cukor] was my last hope of ever enjoying the picture. He was quite right, as the head office suddenly decided that the script (written by one of America's best dramatists) which they had for *two* years wasn't good enough, and started writing one themselves. So you can imagine what the dialogue is like."

The only member of the cast who appeared unaffected was Leslie Howard. Before shooting started, when he made his costume tests, he realized how much he disliked the prospect of playing Ashley. "I hate the damn part," he wrote to his daughter. "I'm not nearly beautiful or young enough for Ashley, and it makes me sick being fixed up to look attractive." As for the film itself: "Terrible lot of nonsense — heaven help me if I ever read the book." When Cukor left, he evidently agreed with most of Hollywood. "David says he is going to sue me for spreading alarm and despondency."

Gable, naturally, involved himself in the question of Cukor's replacement. MGM wanted his successor to be one of their own contract directors, and gave Selznick a list of those available: King Vidor, Robert Z. Leonard, Jack Conway, and Victor Fleming. Selznick asked Gable which of these he would prefer, and the actor immediately chose Fleming, a man with a tough, no-nonsense facade, with whom he had previously worked on several pictures, including *Red Dust* and *Test Pilot*. Selznick, in spite of his mysteriously high opinion of Leonard (an amiable hack who was, in fact, eager to step in), agreed. All this was settled within twenty-four hours.

As well as being a "man's director," Fleming had proved himself a highly competent manager of action and spectacle in a variety of films; but he accepted the job with reluctance, only after pressure from MGM and Gable. He shared the industry's general opinion of the project and still had a few days' work left on minor scenes for his current picture, *The Wizard of Oz*. Raymond Klune remembers him as a dour man, notably foul-mouthed and anti-Semitic. ("How can you keep on working for all these Jews?" he used to ask him.) Lee Garmes also told me that Fleming had been forewarned of Selznick's habit of re-writing the script, and when he was shown the existing footage the producer was shocked by his reaction. "David," he said, "your fucking script is no fucking good."

Nobody having said this before, Selznick felt obliged to make a gesture and agreed to call in a new writer. He turned to his old friend Ben Hecht, a man of occasional and cynical brilliance, famous as a "fixer" of scripts and self-described as "a man of letters with a Hollywood address." He had started as a play-wright, collaborating with Charles MacArthur on *The Front Page* and *Twentieth Century*, then decided ease and affluence were indispensable to life, and began a long career of writing to order. His scripts for Lubitsch (*Design for Living*) and Hitch-cock (*Notorious*) are high points in this; his writing of *Nothing Sacred* in two weeks and rewriting of *Hurricane* for Goldwyn in two days, his most impressive technical feats. Most importantly, he would always make his quick, shrewd mind available so long as the price was right.

In *A Child of the Century* he tells how Selznick and Fleming arrived at his house on a Sunday morning at dawn. By sunrise, the three of them had reached the studio in Selznick's car, terms having been settled on the way. Hecht would be paid $15,000, and all the work had to be done in a week. Then "four Selznick secretaries who had not yet been to sleep that night staggered in with typewriters, paper and a gross of pencils." Appalled to discover that Hecht had never read *Gone With the Wind*, Selznick decided there was no time to remedy that now. Since Fleming hadn't read it either, the producer himself would give Hecht a verbal summary that lasted an hour. "I had seldom heard a more involved plot. My verdict was that nobody could make a sensible movie out of it. Fleming, who was reputed to be part Indian, sat brooding at his own council fires. I asked him if he had been able to follow the story David had told. He said no."

Hecht then asked Selznick if at any time since he bought the novel a writer had turned this "Ouidalike flight into the Civil War" into a workable screen narrative. Selznick seemed at first doubtful; then, remembering Sidney Howard's first draft, long since buried in revisions, he wondered if it might be worth looking at again. A secretary finally located the original and Selznick read it aloud. "Precise and telling," was Hecht's verdict, and saw no problem other than reducing its length. For the rest of the week he worked in eighteen- and twenty-four-hour stretches doing exactly that. Selznick and Fleming acted out the scenes as he edited them, David playing Scarlett and her father, and Fleming reading Rhett and Ashley, the latter a character for whom Hecht felt no sympathy and suggested should be cut. Selznick refused, insisting that Ashley was a "typical southern gentleman." Believing that food slowed up the creative process, the producer limited their lunches to a snack of bananas and salted peanuts. On the fifth day, in the act of eating a banana, he collapsed and had to be revived by a doctor. On the sixth, a blood vessel burst in Fleming's eye. Hecht conserved his strength by dozing on a couch while Selznick and Fleming acted out the scenes, and at the end of the week had completed a revised version of the first half. It was a performance of sheer technique, not invention, and he wanted and took no credit.

Later, Selznick was to play down Hecht's contribution. (He also rewrote it.) He claimed that while Sidney Howard was the only writer who did substantial work on the script, the final structure was eighty percent his own, with the rest conceived by Howard and Jo Swerling; of the dialogue not transcribed or closely adapted from Margaret Mitchell — perhaps a hundred lines in all — he said that most came from himself, with a few lines supplied by Hecht and Van Druten. Then what else did Hecht invent for his $15,000? If we are to believe Selznick, "the construction of one sequence" and the idea of inserting narrative titles, which they wrote together.

Once again this is a matter which cannot be finally settled. However, on the evidence of the finished film, I would say that fifty percent of its structure is due to none of these, but to Margaret Mitchell. Selznick never allowed Howard's first draft to circulate, but from what is known of their conferences, and the memos written to Howard by Selznick, it would seem that Hecht's reaction was entirely sound. The Selznick office had once calculated that to film every page of the book, with the conversation and action as described, would result in a film 168 hours or a week long. Apart from this, *Gone With the Wind* presents no formidable problems to an adapter. Howard's neglected script was at least a monumental act of condensation, and all that really remained was to finish what he had begun. Technically the novel's only fault is its verbosity, something it shares with many of Selznick's memos. It seems likely that Selznick's own temperament had been a major factor in the problem of cutting the script down to size. Never reluctant to use a paragraph instead of a sentence, tending to equate bulk with impressiveness, insisting on literary fidelity, he must have severely inhibited his writers; and his method of working on the script only in sudden, frantic bursts must have made it almost impossible for them to gain a complete hold on the material.

At any rate, whatever Hecht achieved during this manic week apparently satisfied Fleming for the time being.

Shooting resumed on March 1, two weeks after Cukor's dismissal. Selznick wanted to retain most of what Cukor had done, except for the day's work on the Atlanta Bazaar, the opening scene on the porch and Scarlett's walk with her father up the hill from Tara, when he tells her, "Land is the only thing in this world that lasts." He was now dissatisfied with the performances of the Tarleton twins on the porch, and he wanted to improve some of the landscaping around Tara.

It was quickly apparent that Vivien Leigh's relationship with the new director, like Scarlett's with Rhett, would be contentious. Any successor to Cukor would have had a difficult time endearing himself to her, but with Fleming's open declaration of intentions, "I'm going to make this picture a melodrama," she prepared for battle. Nor was she pleased when he immediately nicknamed her "Fiddle-de-Dee." There were to be few moments, in fact, when she wasn't complaining about Selznick's dialogue and the way Fleming expected her to play it. Selznick described later how she would mutter under her breath before a take and make "small moans." Nevertheless she was always polite and professional; they arrived at a workable truce and a grudging respect for each other.

Fleming's character and talents remain something of a mystery, like those of so many Hollywood directors of the '30s. At different times he had been a cameraman, a big-game hunter and an air force pilot; for a while he considered giving up film-making

altogether and going back to shooting tigers. Like Howard Hawks, John Ford, William Wellman, Jack Conway, and many others, he was the product of a period when Hollywood film-making was dominated by the enormously successful organization of the studios, their executives determining the material and their technicians the style of the pictures. "Production" in general dominated "direction." Sam Goldwyn once explained to a reporter that William Wyler "only directed" *Wuthering Heights;* the producer "made" it. After an argument with Eddie Mannix about his way of shooting a scene for MGM's *Queen Christina,* Reuben Mamoulian was warned, "We don't make pictures here, we remake them." Prolific, accepting quite a few routine assignments, these directors also had to fight against being typecast. Lacking the insistent personality of a Chaplin, a Lubitsch or a von Sternberg, it's not surprising that their work seems only at moments individual. Most significantly of all, they were masked. In their lives as well as their movies they put up a smokescreen of masculine comradeship, card-playing, wise-cracking, and took care to play down any image of themselves as artists. In part this was certainly self-protective. An extro-verted doing-the-job approach was always more reassuring to their employers, and it was the front they strove to present.

Fleming's mask seems to have been clamped on for personal reasons as well. Like Clark Gable he comes under the Heming-way syndrome, on the run from sensibility and tenderness be-cause they seemed to him feminine traits, concerned to main-tain a super-virile exterior. In all this he was the opposite of Cukor, whose modesty and humor never concealed a deep in-volvement with his metier. Others remember Fleming with less dislike than Klune, but none with warmth; it is generally agreed that his manner was disagreeable. His long association with Douglas Fairbanks in the '20s, and the partnership with Gable in the '30s, suggests the world in which as a director he was most at home. The favorite director of Selznick's father, Allan Dwan, once congratulated Fleming on his assignment to make *The Mollycoddle* for Fairbanks because the story contained such "clean and decent American characters, clean, courageous, bold, adventurous men and plucky, charming women." In *Gone With the Wind* Fleming would have to discover darker shades in the boldness of Rhett and the pluck of Scarlett.

When Selznick continued rewriting the script in spite of Hecht, and once again more blue pages mingled with the white, Vivien Leigh began to object. At first she had felt deeply discouraged, faced on the one hand with Fleming, a man she considered an expert but simpleminded technician, replacing an artist, a "poor wretch" who had never had time even to read the book, and on the other with the leviathan of Selznick; but in spite of being so young and unknown, she tackled both with a cooly virulent determination. In her loyalty to Cukor's conception of the role, and her arguments with Selznick about the script, she became a creative influence on the picture far beyond the limits of an actress. On the surface de Havilland was pliant, while secretly conferring with Cukor; Gable and Fleming were old friends; Leslie Howard was bored and given to flubbing his lines; it was left to Vivien to speak her mind, which she began to do with a courage and passion that must have astonished Selznick. ("No Pollyanna," he would sigh when describing her.) Every day she would arrive on the set with a copy of the novel in her hand, as evidence that the original was superior to the rewrites, and also "to look up each scene as we filmed it, to remind myself where I was supposed to be, and how I should be feeling — until Selznick shouted at me to throw the damned thing away." Without the book and without Cukor, she said, she would never have been able to get through. But there was also her own strength, and the self-discipline that de Havilland called "not harsh, but of an exquisite order." She had wanted the part, she had started with great hopes and was determined not to lose out now. "She gave something to that film," de Havilland has commented, "which I don't think she ever got back."

It is now known that tuberculosis often has the effect of intensifying its victim's personality, making him more vividly himself. Thomas Mann's *The Magic Mountain* is partly about this, and the lives of many artists (Kafka, D. H. Lawrence, Katherine Mansfield) have illustrated it. Although Vivien's tuberculosis of the lung was not to be diagnosed until five years later, the disease often exists for many years before it declares itself. It is impossible not to wonder if her condition wasn't already formed at the time of *Gone With the Wind*, and already having this effect. All the accounts of her during production — to say nothing of the performance itself — suggest something reckless and feverish beneath her self-control that seems to have astonished everybody. And Lydia Schiller, one of Selznick's production secretaries and a continuity girl on the film, remembers Olivier being stunned by her performance when Selznick screened the picture for him during the shooting of *Rebecca*. Next day on the set, he remarked to Miss Schiller, "I never knew she had it in her." The same observer also described to me Vivien's reactions at two different moments which reflect the heightened contradictions in her nature. In the scene where Scarlett leaves the hospital to find the long-range cannons already pounding Atlanta, she vehemently refused the offer of a double for any of the shots, and for each camera angle walked fearless through the bombardment, dummy shells exploding only a few feet away. At the end of Part One, she objected violently to the idea of retching after Scarlett plucks the radish from the earth and crams it in her mouth; the detail struck her as inelegant. It took Selznick half an hour to talk her into it.

Two more letters to her husband show the transition from

despair to tenacity. March 13: "It is really very miserable and going terribly slowly. I am such a *fool* to have done it." April 2: "The part has now become the greatest responsibility one can imagine. . . . As far as the film goes, it creeps along — very long hours and very little work done — principally I think because every scene is so hard to play because of the appalling dialogue. However, David Selznick promises me that Sidney Howard is coming back on the script."

This promise was not really kept; Howard came out to California for a few days to rework a couple of scenes in Part Two, and that was all. (A month after the end of the shooting he was run over by a tractor in an accident on his Connecticut farm and died.) So the battle of the pages continued. Vivien always liked to find a line or a speech that she considered a talisman for understanding, a key to the character; and she became obsessed by an avowal from Scarlett when Rhett proposes marriage to her after Frank Kennedy's death. She's been drinking, and tells Rhett she's glad her mother has died and can't see her now. "She brought me up to be so kind, and thoughtful, just like her, and I've turned out such a disappointment." Selznick revised this scene several times, usually cutting out the line. She would demand that he put it back, and it was there when Fleming finally shot the scene. (In the same way, while filming *A Streetcar Named Desire*, she felt that Kazan had thrown away a key line about Blanche in her youth, spoken by her sister — "She was so tender and trusting" — and insisted he reshoot the scene.) Fleming tended to see women as either good or bad, and he saw Scarlett as bad, so that Vivien constantly felt he was trying to make her "just a terrible bitch." Never an actress to flinch from unsympathetic moments, she accused Fleming of always ignoring Scarlett's vulnerable side. But, as she wrote to her husband, the only direction she ever received was, "Ham it up!"

With Gable her relations were polite but formal. He was Fleming's friend, and therefore on the opposite side; also, the two men had much in common. One of the great screen personalities of his time, Gable never lost a fear of exposing himself. Cast as the male conqueror, adored for it, he was in life sexually cautious, and until he met Carole Lombard drawn to older women. In his early career as an actor in touring companies, he played with several distinguished, middle-aged and lecherous ladies of the theater. Both Alice Brady and Jane Cowl tried unsuccessfully to seduce him; Pauline Frederick got as far as persuading him to rub her back after the performance. Even though he complained that Miss Frederick looked at him as if she never expected to see another man in her life, his first two marriages were to women considerably older than himself. "You know I love Pappy," Lombard once remarked after their marriage, "even though he's not the greatest lay." And for years it was a closely guarded studio secret that he wore false teeth.

Anxious to improve himself as an actor, Gable was equally anxious that no one should know about it. Self-consciousness haunted him, diffidence held him back. If a director stopped him in the middle of a take, he could be paralyzed. Unable to pick up lines quickly, he had to go back to the beginning and get into the scene all over again. Over the years he struggled to acquire technique. At MGM this was well known, and his screen personality would be carefully built up to exploit all that was appealing in him, roles were chosen that gave him the fewest problems, directors found who knew how to relax him best. Happiest in scenes of action and wise-cracking, when he had to threaten sexuality rather than demonstrate it, Rhett Butler was the first part in which he knew he'd have to explore himself. Vivien quickly sensed his nervousness, and ironically the newcomer found herself reassuring the famous star. Impressed but wary, he withdrew to the camaraderie of Fleming. There was no

one else in the company whom he really trusted. Tense when he began the picture — the role intimidated him and his divorce case was coming to court in a few weeks' time * — he was also a naturally suspicious man. Selznick noted that on several occasions the actor accused him of trying to "do him in."

It seems likely that the relationship of Vivien and Gable outside the film contributed something important to their scenes together. In the novel, Rhett is amused by Scarlett because he knows that her airs and graces conceal a very hard, level head; physically attracted to her, he also knows that in spite of her denials she feels the same way. In the film, something more happens. For the first time Rhett is confronted by a woman as strong as himself, and there are moments when you detect a guarded, almost rueful quality beneath the swagger. (It was there in all of Gable's performances.) Each has called the other's bluff, and the marriage develops into a fluctuating struggle for power. When Rhett walks out, he is confessing in a way that he's lost. The resonance comes from their personal chemistry as performers.

The most difficult scene for Gable to play, in the picture and in his whole career, was when Melanie breaks the news to Rhett of Scarlett's miscarriage. The facade of the man dissolves. "Melanie had never seen a man cry and of all men, Rhett, so suave, so mocking, so eternally sure of himself." The idea seemed as chilling to Gable as it did to Melanie. He pleaded with Fleming to have the scene rewritten, or to cheat it, not to make him play it, even threatening to walk off the picture and give up his career. Perhaps only Fleming could have handled the problem. One of the reasons that Gable liked him was that he always appeared to defer to the star; to the others he would give orders, but to Gable he would say, "Do you think we can try it this way?" Fleming discussed the problem with Selznick first, and

---

* Rhea Langham Gable is reported to have settled for $265,000.

the producer partially relieved Gable by promising to shoot the scene two ways: with tears, and with an eloquently turned back. Then, privately, Fleming suggested to Gable that the tears would be much better; they would not destroy his image (as he feared), but increase the audience's sympathy for the character. A friend as well as a director, he knew the way to get to him. He shot the dry-eyed version first, and then — after a last protest from the star — the weeping. The weeping was used, of course, and on the screen shows no strain or hesitation. Even though he never attempted anything as complex again, Rhett remains the part with which Gable is most identified. Fleming's most important

contribution to *Gone With the Wind* was his personal knowledge of the actor, and his ability to release him.

Three weeks after the picture resumed shooting, another important head fell. Lee Garmes was conferring with Cameron Menzies on an elaborate shot in which Scarlett makes her way through the hundreds of Confederate wounded at the Atlanta railroad station. Like many other spectacular moments, it was to be executed under Selznick's close supervision. He had demanded 2,500 extras for the soldiers, an unheard-of number in those days, and the Screen Extras Guild had only 1,500 available. Seizing the opportunity to save money, Selznick ordered 1,000 dummies to swell the crowd, insisting that the trick be kept a secret. (Years later, when a journalist asked him if it were true that dummies had been used in the scene, he refused to say. Unwilling to lie, the producer of *A Star Is Born* simply could not betray his romantic notion that to divulge professional secrets detracted from the "glamor" of the movies.) He also wanted the camera to follow Scarlett on a crane which could be raised a hundred feet above the ground for panoramic effect. No studio had a crane large enough, and the shot was postponed until Ray Klune had the idea of borrowing one from a construction company, then building a concrete ramp, so that its smoothness of movement when mounted was assured. Rehearsals for this took several days, with a specially detailed additional crew. By the time everything was ready, Garmes had been taken off the picture. Viewing and reviewing the dailies, as he always did, Selznick had come to the conclusion that his cameraman's use of color was too "neutral" for his taste.

"We were using a new type of film," Garmes has explained, "with softer tones, softer quality, but David had been accustomed to working with picture postcard colors. He tried to blame me because the picture was looking too quiet in texture. I liked the look; I thought it was wonderful." In the first half hour of the picture, above all in the scenes at the Wilkes barbecue, Garmes's images subtly blend tones and shades, rather than primary colors, and are far ahead of anything else being done at the time; yet it was the Twelve Oaks sequence that Selznick particularly complained about in a memo to Fleming and Klune: "We should have seen beautiful reds and blues and yellows and greens in costumes so designed that the audience would have gasped at their beauty." (He told Garmes later that he realized he had been wrong about this.) According to the Technicolor adviser, Ray Rennahan, Garmes's lighting was "softer" and "flatter" than the style Selznick wanted; Rennahan's own preference was for more sharpness, and he recommended a cameraman, Ernest Haller, who was fortunately ready to take over at a day's notice; so this changeover was made without any loss of time. Haller had never done a color film before, but with Rennahan's guidance he achieved a greater "definition," and Selznick expressed himself pleased with the result. But the difference in style, which will be discussed later, was far less than might have been expected.

The next major crisis occurred a month later. By the middle of April, Selznick was worried by what he described as Fleming's physical and mental exhaustion. Fleming's doctor had assured him there was no cause for alarm, and until April 26 the director continued to work efficiently on the film, though he alternated between an almost despairing energy and violent explosions of rage. After another disagreement with Vivien while rehearsing a scene, he threw down his script, walked out of the studio, and drove home to Malibu. Next day it was reported that he'd had a nervous collapse and had told his wife he'd contemplated suicide, wanting to plunge his car over a cliff from the coast highway.

Unable to reach him by phone, Selznick contacted his doctor and learned that the breakdown was feigned; Fleming was certainly tired and angry, but not in the least a hospital case. According to Klune, only he and Selznick knew about this. It was decided to withhold the information from the rest of the company. From what both Klune and Lydia Schiller have told me, it is not difficult to understand the reasons for Fleming's sudden theatrical gesture. It was a protest against what he considered David's domination of the picture. From the time Fleming took over, the continuity girl was under orders from Selznick to report any deviation on the set from the shooting plan or the script. Fleming constantly received memos about his use of color (comparing it unfavorably to the color in *The Garden of Allah*), about padding Vivien's bosom (referred to as "the breastwork situation"), and about the costumes. Fleming's request for the schedule to be rearranged so that he could shoot in continuity was refused; Selznick told him it was impossible to keep Gable on the payroll doing nothing. Probably the peak of his aggravation was reached after Selznick had screened *The Great Waltz*, an MGM picture about Johann Strauss, credited to Julien Duvivier, but for which Fleming had shot some major sequences. Highly impressed with its technique, Selznick asked the director why his work on *Gone With the Wind* was so much less remarkable. Fleming blamed the cumbersome Technicolor equipment, explaining that on a black-and-white movie he had far more flexibility with camera angles. In all these confrontations Fleming was the loser; he finally threw a tantrum and converted it into a breakdown, under the false impression that Selznick would promise to reduce the pressure if he came back.

Discussing the situation with Klune, the producer said that the best way to get Fleming back would be to replace him. The fact that the breakdown was feigned made the crisis no less severe, and it was imperative that shooting not be closed down again. There was enough work to occupy a second unit for a few days, and the famous crane shot of the Atlanta wounded was now ready to be made. (Cameron Menzies and Ray Rennahan executed it during Fleming's absence.) Selznick's first choice for a replacement was again Robert Z. Leonard, who turned out to be unavailable; Klune suggested Sam Wood, who had just finished *Goodbye, Mr. Chips* in England and was now in New York. Over the long-distance phone he accepted the assignment, and began working three days later.

Perhaps the fact that Wood had once worked as assistant to De Mille led Selznick to believe that he could tackle a story of this size. The rest of his mainly routine work — of which the high points had been two Marx Brothers films and the Gladys George version of *Madame X* — could hardly have done so. Up to this time, all of Sam Wood's movies had been remarkable for their complete lack of visual appeal. No doubt Selznick relied on Menzies to take care of this, and an interesting minor footnote to film history follows. Wood came under the spell of Menzies, and a year later they worked together on *Our Town*, then on two very stylish period pieces, *Kings' Row* and *Ivy*. Throughout the '40s, in fact, the movies directed by Sam Wood display an increasingly elaborate visual surface. Before *Gone With the Wind* his work had no personality, though his direction of actors was competent; but afterward it at least had some in the way it looked.

In relation to *Gone With the Wind*, the minor footnote clinches a major point. From the time that Sam Wood took over, Selznick became explicitly *the* creator of the film, in all but name its director and writer as well as producer. The machine he had built for this purpose now operated for him alone. Actors excepted, it had no irreplaceable parts. If a cameraman failed to deliver the hoped-for images, if a director temporarily threw in the sponge, it became simply a matter of calling for a new component. For the rest of his life Selznick was to approach film-making in this way, and his later projects were notorious for the clashes with directors and technicians, the numbers of scenes rewritten and reshot. It explains Cukor's remark that *Gone With the Wind*, in spite of its success, contained the seeds of Selznick's destruction. Creating it, he was at the same time taking the first steps toward destroying himself. Convinced that his talents were protean, he was able on this one occasion to stretch them to extraordinary limits; but he drew the wrong conclusion when he believed it could happen again.

Fleming "recovered" after two weeks, and it is characteristic that Selznick brought him back while still retaining Sam Wood. He had devised an elaborate system to make up for lost time. Confident from the first that Fleming would return, he placated Gable by promising him that none of his scenes would be directed by Wood; he persuaded Vivien and the other principals to work for both directors as the schedule demanded; he stepped up the number of second units for incidental shots to five, and entrusted Menzies with two major sequences, as well as several linking passages. Amazingly, there is no disparity in styles in the resulting scenes, unlike the variations of Selznick's later *Duel in the Sun*, which went through three directors and three cameramen, and shows it. Not only were Fleming and Wood in effect working as megaphones for Selznick, but Menzies now coordinated the visual aspects of every sequence even more closely, and the memos continued to arrive whenever Selznick heard that one of his directors had changed a camera set-up. In this way, displacements of personnel could not affect the look and construction of the whole. The only variable could have been the actors, frequently informed what age they would be playing only twenty-four hours beforehand; but they not only survived, they never lost faith. The greatest burden fell on Vivien Leigh and Olivia de Havilland, who would find themselves week after week shooting a scene for Sam Wood in the morning, then moving to Fleming's set in the afternoon for the filming of an episode several years later (or earlier). Vivien said later that she had "no time to let worry get the upper hand. I lived Scarlett for almost six months from early morning till late at night." Olivia de Havilland has told me that she remembers "very little sense of dislocation, because of David Selznick's astonishingly unifying influence." She never doubted that they were making "something special, something which would last forever."

It could only have been Selznick who enabled Sam Wood to pass a difficult test, winning approval from the actors on the first scene he directed. It happened at night, de Havilland remembers, on the back lot, after dinner, "the moment when Vivien and I come out of the church and are accosted on its steps by Belle Watling. I liked that scene, and thought it went well, and was relieved to see that the new hand would guide us wisely." There was also a debt of which Sam Wood was probably unaware: both actresses had been fortified by discussing the scene beforehand with Cukor.

Leslie Howard was also finding himself under pressure. Contracted to star in *Intermezzo* as well as become its associate producer, he was now requested to play two roles simultaneously; the starting date of *Intermezzo* could not be delayed even though *Gone With the Wind* was behind schedule. Having disagreed with the original director, William Wyler, over the script, Selznick had lined up Gregory Ratoff to replace him. (There was no time, of course, for Howard to perform any of the duties of associate producer, which is what had originally interested him.) He accepted the situation with his usual detached whimsy, remarking to Klune that he didn't mind being given only fifteen minutes to switch roles, but would have liked more time for the costume change.

During all these months of tense and upstream work, Selznick the autocrat was not the only key figure. There was also Selznick the personal charmer and enthusiast, magnetic and in spite of everything irresistible. Besieged, drugged, chain-smoking, sleepless, he seemed possessed of infinite patience in personal matters as well, and had the knack of making the people who worked for him (Fleming excepted) feel that they were loved. Even those upon whom the ax fell displayed surprisingly little bitterness — Garmes worked for him again, and he was to remain friends with Cukor. "He treated us with such appreciation," de Havilland remembers. "At the end of every week you'd find a packet of eight-by-ten glossy stills of the scenes you'd worked on waiting in your dressing room. You'd do anything for a man like that." The six-foot-one figure with his ponderous frame and rather clumsy movements was a genuine source of wonder. Whatever he did had an aura of such conviction that it seemed curiously innocent. In a sense it was, since all his actions were based on the very simple idea that any methods were justified to make *Gone With the Wind* come out the way he wanted. The hostility of the industry in general now worked in his favor. "Turkey" and "bust" and "white elephant" and "Selznick's folly" were the favorite epithets, and they had the effect of intensifying the loyalty of his actors and technicians. When he remarked, "There's only room for one prima donna on this lot, and that's me," they not only knew it to be true but savored the jovial confidence with which he said it. They also learned that the unceasing notes of complaints, the hesitations and endless rewriting, reflected a desire to extract the best from himself as well as others. According to Garmes, while David thought he knew what he wanted, he frequently had trouble recognizing it when he saw it; according to Klune, even when he was satisfied he wondered whether there might not be a better way of doing it. Taken together, these comments add up to a very workable definition of a perfectionist.

In the photographs of Selznick from his youth to his early sixties there is one constant: his smile. Lighted by pleasure, the face suddenly belongs to a small boy. The moment of triumph appears to astonish him. It is the mark of the true showman to be able to amaze himself, and the dismissals, frictions, and breakdowns all became unimportant when he viewed the footage that had been shot each day and, like God creating the world, finally saw that it was good.

Approaching the role of Rhett Butler as a movie star, Gable had one basic problem: to the public he personified the role, but to himself he didn't. Fleming, professional ally and personal friend, was there to help him resolve it. Vivien approached Scarlett as an actress, and on her own. She had secret support and help from Cukor, but on the set she always pressured herself by insisting on seeing the film as a whole. Working from sixteen to eighteen hours every day, with only four days throughout the entire shooting when she was not on call, she had also to reconcile professional conscience with an increasing desire to get to the end of it and escape. During the last ten weeks of shooting Olivier was in New York, having completed *Wuthering Heights* and agreed to play in the theater opposite Katharine Cornell in *No Time for Comedy*. Vivien had always been the exile in the cast; she still did not like Hollywood; the loneliness of separation became intense. Every Sunday that she went to Cukor's house now, she would talk as much about wanting to go to New York as about the role itself. Yet she never "settled." Cukor tells how one day in early June she arrived as usual at his house, took a swim, then lay down and fell into a long deep sleep. When she woke up, she giggled suddenly and told him, "I was an absolute bitch on the set yesterday." They had been shooting the scene with Ashley that she'd played in the test with Douglass Montgomery standing in for Leslie Howard, and she felt it wasn't right. After another of their arguments, she made "poor old Fleming trot over and screen the test." In spite of this, she didn't quite recapture the power of the first version; but by this time, under the circumstances, it was probably impossible.

On June 27 Fleming shot the last scene of the picture, the first that Margaret Mitchell had actually written. It had not existed in script form until the day before. The problem of how to convey that Scarlett, after Rhett leaves her, still believes she can get him back and realizes that even if she doesn't she can always return to Tara, had defeated every writer. Selznick came up at the last moment with the idea of Scarlett addressing another soliloquy to the camera, speaking lines selected from the novel's inner monologue, added to which would be the disembodied voices of her father and Ashley reminding her of "the red earth of Tara." The producer records that "it was pretty loudly jeered at on paper," but that preview audiences found it gave the ending "a tremendous lift." They missed, however, Rhett's final line, "Frankly, my dear, I don't give a damn," which was to become one of the most quoted in the film, like Scarlett's "I won't think about it today; I'll think about it tomorrow." It seems incredible now that the line was only permitted after months of negotiation with the Hays Office, but at that time the word "damn" was completely taboo. In his original draft Sidney Howard changed the line, after consultation with Selznick, to "Frankly, my dear, I don't care." The scene was shot both ways, but it was not until the end of November — after Selznick's repeated pleas that he'd be unmercifully mocked for omitting the famous phrase, and that the dictionary definition of the terrible word was no worse than "a vulgarism" — that the censors finally granted permission.

In the novel, Rhett's line is "My dear, I don't give a damn," but Howard's added "Frankly" was left in, a minor yet incalculable improvement that would probably never have occurred by design.

By July 1 some final scenes with bit players had been completed, and shooting was officially over. Vivien's departure for New York was delayed by Selznick, who wanted yet another retake on the opening porch scene. It still dissatisfied him, though he couldn't say why. Then, gazing at Vivien's face, he exclaimed "My God, you look old!" "You'd look old, too," she answered, "if you'd been working eighteen hours a day for weeks on end." She was too indignant to notice that between the beginning and the end of shooting Selznick's black curly hair had become faintly streaked with grey.

In the last week of August Vivien returned for the retake. Seven months older, but looking sixteen again, Scarlett is back on the summery porch in innocent white. This time Sam Wood directed the scene on one of those perfect untroubled afternoons that ought to last forever, and Scarlett refuses to believe the talk of war. Next day, the actress joined Olivier on Ronald Colman's yacht. Over the Labor Day weekend, time was suspended just as it had been on the porch at Tara. Then they heard on the radio that England had declared war on Germany.

six

A PAUSE
FOR VITAL
STATISTICS

R AY RENNAHAN HAS ESTIMATED that Victor Fleming actually directed 40 percent of *Gone With the Wind*; Raymond Klune puts it at "possibly" as high as 50 percent. It would be fair, I think, to split the difference. At one time Selznick considered including a title card acknowledging the work of George Cukor and Sam Wood, but neither of them wanted it, and Fleming fiercely protested the idea.

The various contributions, with percentages of the total footage, can be broken down as follows:

Fleming (45%): all the scenes with Rhett Butler, except his visit to Aunt Pittypat's when he presents Scarlett with the Paris hat. These include, in Part One, the Wilkes barbecue, the Atlanta Bazaar, the escape from Atlanta; in Part Two, all the scenes with Rhett and Scarlett. He also directed Scarlett returning to Tara and discovering that her mother has died, and Scarlett in the fields at the end of Part One; the opening sequences of Part Two, with Scarlett taking charge of Tara, Scarlett's second declaration of love to Ashley when he returns from the War, and Scarlett at Melanie's deathbed.

Sam Wood (15%): in Part One, Belle Watling accosting Melanie and Scarlett outside the church, and Ashley returning on leave from the War — Scarlett's jealousy of him and Melanie, and his description of the doomed Confederate army; in Part Two, Scarlett going to Atlanta in search of Rhett, excluding the scene with Rhett, but including the glimpses of Reconstruction and the meeting with Frank Kennedy, culminating in his proposal of marriage; all the scenes at Kennedy's sawmill, notably when Scarlett persuades Ashley to stay and work with her, and India Wilkes's discovery of their embrace; Scarlett in the red dress at Melanie's party; the first half (up to Rhett's entrance) of the sequence in which Scarlett, Melanie, and the others wait for Ashley and Kennedy to return from the raid on Shanty Town, in which Kennedy is killed; and Mammy's account to Melanie on the staircase, of life in the Butler household since the death of Bonnie Blue.

Cameron Menzies (15%, possibly more when one includes many incidental shots): Scarlett and Melanie tending the wounded at the hospital, beginning and ending with their shadows on the wall; Scarlett in the streets of Atlanta during the bombardment, up to Rhett's arrival; the crowd waiting in the square for the casualty lists; Scarlett's return to Tara, through the enemy lines, after Rhett abandons her outside Atlanta. He also devised all the montage sequences — glimpses of the defeated Confederate army and so on — and, in Selznick's words, laid out camera angles, lighting effects, and other visual details "for which he will never be adequately credited."

Cukor (5%): Mammy lacing up Scarlett for the barbecue, Rhett arriving at Aunt Pittypat's with the hat for Scarlett, Scarlett and Prissy delivering Melanie's baby, and Scarlett shooting the Union deserter at Tara. The final "authorship" of the opening porch scene, which was reshot three times, remains in doubt.

It is probably a mixture of Cukor's second version and the Fleming retake.

Reeves Eason, the chief second unit director (2%): many incidental shots, and Scarlett's ride through Shanty Town and the attack on her by the Negro, done on location near Big Bear, California.

Of the famous "pull-back" shots, Fleming directed only one, at the end of Part One, after Scarlett has vowed never to go hungry again. The first pull-back in the picture, from Scarlett and her father on the hill at sunset, with Tara in the distance, and the crane shot of the wounded soldiers at the railroad station, were done by Cameron Menzies.

The remaining 18% of the footage is made up of work by

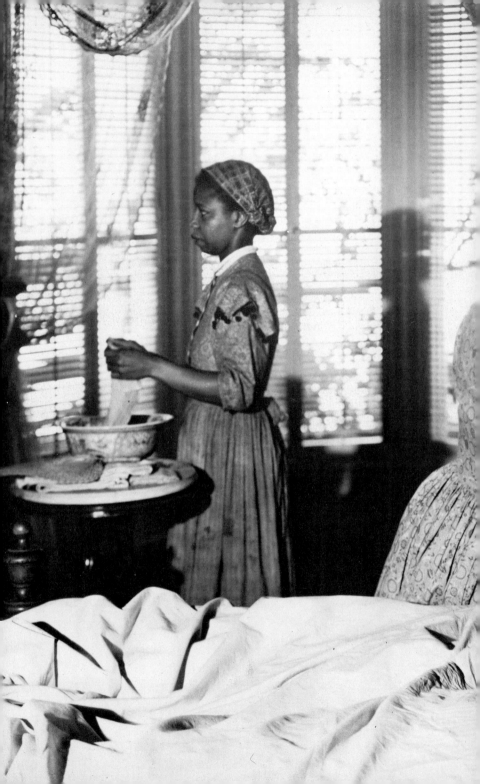

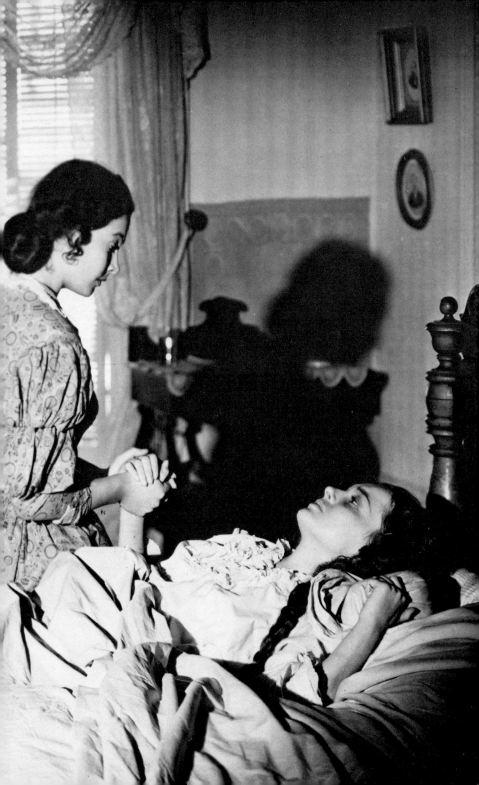

various second units, establishing shots, "run-throughs" — arrivals in carriages and so on — and process shots.

Ernest Haller received sole credit for the photography, although Lee Garmes was responsible for most of the first hour of the picture, and all Cukor's scenes. All sequences directed by Cameron Menzies were done with Ray Rennahan, who also created the master shots for the burning of Atlanta.

Selznick considered another title card acknowledging the work of Jo Swerling and Ben Hecht on the script, then decided against it, as he felt that no one except Sidney Howard (who received sole credit) and himself made a really substantial contribution. On the program for the Atlanta premiere he singled out for special appreciation Victor Fleming, Cameron Menzies, Jack Cosgrove, the director of special effects, and the editor Hal Kern, and Kay Brown, "the very first to recognize the film possibilities of the novel."

Preparation period: 250,000 man hours. *Production period:* 750,000 man hours. Burning of Atlanta filmed December 10, 1938. Principal photography began January 26, 1939, and concluded July 1, 1939. (Shooting was closed down for twelve days after Cukor left the picture.)

Footage: 449,512 feet of film shot, and 160,000 printed. *Final running time:* 20,300 feet (222 minutes). Approximate ratio of film shot to film used: 20 to 1.

Cast: Fifty-nine leading and supporting characters, 2,400 extras. The supporting characters, from Hattie McDaniel down, were paid a total of $10,000.

Animal extras: 1,100 horses and 375 assorted pigs, mules, oxen, cows, and dogs.

Vehicles used: a total of 450 wagons, ambulances, and gun caissons.

Design: Cameron Menzies, with Macmillan Johnson, created 3,000 sketches covering all the major scenes in the film, and designed 200 sets. Ninety sets were actually built, executed by Lyle Wheeler, using 1,000,000 feet of lumber.

Wardrobe: Walter Plunkett created 5,500 separate items. Total cost: $153,818. Laundry cost during shooting: $10,000.

Set dressing: Thirty-four different carpet designs, 36 wallpaper designs, handpainted — and for the scene of the Atlanta Bazaar alone, 10,000 manufactured articles.

Actual production cost: $3,700,000. *Total cost,* with added overheads of prints, publicity, etcetera: $4,250,000. Of this,

$1,250,000 was invested by MGM, the rest by backers of Selznick International.

To date, the gross of *Gone With the Wind* on the world market approaches $120,000,000. It has not yet been shown on television.

seven

HOME

S HOOTING COMPLETED, Selznick moved on with his usual relentless energy. He began not only to supervise the montages, the process shots and the editing, but to keep a frequently complaining eye on production of *Rebecca*, which started just as *Gone With the Wind* ended. There was also the final cut of *Intermezzo* to be approved, and a publicity campaign to launch Ingrid Bergman as a Hollywood star. On *Rebecca*, Selznick disagreed as repeatedly with its director as he had with Victor Fleming, but this time found himself up against a master antagonist. Forewarned of his producer's taste for interference, Hitchcock applied his personal methods of filmmaking with such economy that the picture could only be edited the way he shot it. He received a number of memos with anguished references to "cutting your film in the camera."

Fortunately no doubt for Hitchcock, the major part of Selznick's time was spent on the task of reducing the thirty hours of printed film for *Gone With the Wind* to around four. With his editor, Hal Kern, Kern's associate, James Newcom, and two production assistants, Barbara Keon and Lydia Schiller, he would dominate sessions that often ran far into the night. His disregard for established time occasionally turned them into an experience reminiscent of the marathon dance contests. A single conference could last for forty-eight uninterrupted hours.

The mass of footage in no way intimidated him. On the contrary, like some Hollywood directors, notably George Stevens and William Wyler, he believed in "protection," preferring a variety of takes and angles from which to choose. All of his films (except, because of Hitchcock's cunning, *Rebecca*) were shot this way, just as their scripts were usually compiled from a mass of different versions; the only difference with *Gone With the Wind* was of degree. He even ordered a retake and some additional shots, dissatisfied yet again with the opening scene on the porch and feeling the need for an extra episode during Scarlett's escape to Tara after the burning of Atlanta. For this, Cameron Menzies created a new sequence in which Scarlett hid the wagon under a bridge at night and Union soldiers passed overhead in a rainstorm.

Because of the state of the script, so heavily annotated, revised, and overrun with temporary pages, Selznick found it increasingly difficult to compare what was edited on the screen with what had been written on paper. Two-thirds of the way through, he ordered Lydia Schiller to view the edited material on a moviola and reconstruct a "final" script from it. The whole thing back in his head again, he was able to assemble a first cut within less than two months, ready for the verdict of Mayer and other MGM executives. The running time was about four hours and twenty-five minutes. Skeptical when he heard about the length, the Emperor was converted by what he saw, and knew that his instincts as showman and businessman had paid off. For a minimum of investment and a maximum share of profits, there was no doubt that the company had a blockbuster on its hands. Repeating his favorite accolade to himself — "Nobody can say I'm not shrewd" — he disagreed only with Selznick's idea of showing the film in two parts, with a fifteen-minute intermission, which meant that theaters could not conveniently run three performances a day. No immediate decision was taken on this, but the fact that Mayer had been obliged to go to the men's room more than once during the screening was later to provide Selznick with effective ammunition.

By early September, Selznick had trimmed forty-five minutes from the first cut, and the film had found what was to be its final length. Max Steiner was already at work on the music; goaded by Selznick, he completed three hours of it in as many months. His discovery that Selznick had also commissioned an "insurance" score from Herbert Stothart in case the deadline wasn't met spurred him, as the producer happily noted, "to faster and greater efforts." This master of the symphonic score, with his taste for huge orchestras and emphatic emotional comment on the action, could at times achieve something approaching restraint (as in *The Letter*), but this was not to be one of them. Selznick liked to saturate his pictures with music (Hitchcock was later to complain about this on *Spellbound*), and he liked the music sweepingly romantic. "If you will just go mad with *schmaltz* in the last three reels," Selznick suggested — but in fact the composer gave him incessant and richly textured sounds throughout; following his usual practice of writing "themes" — one for Scarlett, one for Rhett, one for Melanie and Ashley, and so on — he came up with a notable winner in "Tara," later adapted for a popular song, "My Own True Love." Much of the rest was skillfully compiled from Civil War songs, *Marching through Georgia*, *Dixie*, *The Bonnie Blue Flag*, and various Stephen Foster tunes. Quintessential Hollywood "prestige" music, the score fits Selznick's conception perfectly, narcotic, quivering, or rousing as occasion demands.

The first two previews were held in Santa Barbara and Riverside at the end of September, a few days apart. In both cases procedure was basically the same. The title of the movie, as usual, was not divulged in advance; at Santa Barbara, before the curtains parted, the theater manager told the audience it was about to see a "very special" picture, and that no one would be allowed to leave once it had started. Guards were posted in the lobby throughout the screening, for Selznick didn't wish any word of the preview to leak out to the press. The manager also informed the audience that the picture would run longer than usual, and proclaimed a delay of fifteen minutes before it started, so that his patrons could telephone families and baby-sitters from the guarded lobby, warning them of a late return home.

When the main title came on the screen, there were excited gasps and cheers. Many people rose to their feet and applauded, as they did at the end, three hours and forty-five minutes later, without intermission. Selznick was moved to tears by the enthusiasm. At Riverside he took the stage personally to introduce the picture; and with the same procedure, on a sweltering heat-wave night, there were no complaints about the length. Selznick described the reactions on the preview cards as "probably the most amazing any picture has ever had." It was here that he won his case for the intermission. Remembering his father-in-law's journeys at the MGM screening, he had a member of his staff check how many people left during the movie for the patrolled rest rooms. Activity was intense enough for the point to be taken.

Victor Fleming, otherwise occupied with the final cutting of *The Wizard of Oz*, which had been delayed until he was free again, was not involved with the editing. (Selznick always kept his directors out of the cutting room.) Never confident about the success of the movie, and still nursing grudges against Selznick, he saw at Riverside its unmistakable triumph. Elated, he was pleasant to Selznick and began talking about it as "his" picture

— a serious mistake, as he was shortly to discover. The estrangement between the two men would soon become final.

Since the discarded footage of *Gone With the Wind* no longer exists, it is impossible to know exactly what was lost in the cutting room between the first MGM screening and the final version shown at the previews. The surviving script material provides no clue. It includes Sidney Howard's first draft; various rewrites of individual scenes; and Fitzgerald's pages, discovered in the Princeton Library by Aaron Latham while doing research for his book, *Crazy Sundays*, about Fitzgerald in Hollywood. The so-called "final" shooting script dated January 24, 1939. On its cover the director is listed as Victor Fleming — but this was two days before Cukor actually started shooting the picture, so it is obviously based on the version assembled and edited by Lydia Schiller *after* the cuts were made. It contains no scenes and only a few lines of dialogue not included in the movie as shown, and is the same script, handsomely bound in leather and illustrated with stills, that Selznick presented to members of the cast and crew before the premiere in Atlanta. With his dislike of revealing professional secrets, he cut the footage from the script as well as the film before releasing it.

Around the cutting of legendary movies, legends grow up. Some private collector is always alleged to own a print of *Greed* more complete than anyone else's, and rumors persist that a pirated, intact version of Cukor's *A Star Is Born* is hidden somewhere in Los Angeles. In the case of *Gone With the Wind* it is said that an assistant editor, angered by the cuts, made off secretly with all the discarded scenes, which are preserved in a remote suburb of the San Fernando Valley. The quest for these promised riches has been no more successful than the search for the Maltese Falcon. Another legend is that the version of *Gone With the Wind* shown at the previews was four and half or five hours long, but the records disprove it. Hal Kern, who edited many of Selznick's pictures and worked closely with him throughout *Gone With the Wind*, has told me that it suffered proportionately fewer cuts than any other production on which he was involved; and Raymond Klune bears this out. Considering the amount of material involved, Kern remembers it as one of the "smoothest and quickest" jobs of his life. After the final version was agreed upon, MGM sales executives again pressured Selznick to shorten it further, for the sake of an extra daily showing, and Selznick asked Kern to see what he could do. His editor labored for three more weeks, then told Selznick that in his opinion any further cuts would obviously harm the picture. "We had these three things — the War, the stories of Scarlett and Rhett, and Melanie and Ashley — and there was nothing more you could take out without losing something important from one of them." Selznick agreed with him, and the idea was abandoned.

Knowing Selznick's habit of requesting "protection" from his directors, of rewriting scenes the day before they were filmed, and the wordiness of his dialogue, it seems certain that the basic cuts were made by eliminating unnecessary background shots, shortening entrances and departures, and trimming the dialogue in existing scenes. (Much of the original mass of extra footage, of course, consisted of multiple prints of the same take, from which Selznick made his final choices.) A good example of a dialogue cut occurs in the exchange between Scarlett and Ashley in Part Two, when they reflect how their lives have altered since the War. Ashley says, "Yes, we've traveled a long road since the old days, haven't we, Scarlett?" Selznick had added some fairly unspeakable lines to this; originally Ashley went on, "Oh, the lazy days, the warm, still country twilights. . . . The high, soft, Negro laughter from the quarters. . . . The golden warmth and

146

security of those days!" We can be sure this is only one of many instances.

Nobody I have questioned remembers any scene that was shot then later bodily removed. Ray Klune agrees with Hal Kern that the footage lost between the first cut and the final print contained only extra dialogue and action within existing scenes. Vivien Leigh could recall only constant battles over dialogue that Selznick had added or rewritten, and his fondness for "speeches" when a line or two could make the point much more effectively. Like the other actors, she never read the whole of Sidney Howard's first script, receiving only individual scenes as Selznick approved them.

The date of the Atlanta premiere was fixed for December 15, 1939. As usual, Selznick's preparations were fastidiously detailed. MGM, as the releasing company, was officially in charge of the ceremonies, but memos, often in cable form, would arrive at the house of their publicity director, Howard Dietz, day and night. "I WANT YOU TO BE VERY CAREFUL OF THE PAPER YOU SELECT FOR THE PROGRAM — stop — SOMETIMES THEIR CRACKLING NOISE MAKES IT DIFFICULT TO HEAR THE DIALOGUE — stop — PROMISE YOU WILL ATTEND TO THIS."

Almost a million people poured into the city. They knew they had no hope of getting seats for the premiere, but were hungry for a glimpse of the stars. The governor of Georgia proclaimed the day of the opening an official state holiday, and the mayor of Atlanta arranged three days of parades and celebrations, urging his citizens to wear period costumes in the streets. Old hoop skirts and beaver hats were enthusiastically dusted off. The facade of the Grand Theatre was fronted with false pillars, to resemble Twelve Oaks. Since it seated only 2,500, tickets (at $10 a head) were at a premium. Besieged by important constituents who would be useful at the next election, the mayor begged

ABOVE: Jock Whitney, Irene Selznick, Olivia de Havilland, David Selznick, Vivien Leigh, and Laurence Olivier arrive at the Atlanta premiere. BELOW: The Atlanta festivities — Olivia de Havilland is apparently not amused.

Vivien Leigh, Clark Gable, Margaret Mitchell, David Selznick, Olivia de Havilland at a party following the premiere of the movie.

MGM for help; he was luckier than the DAR, whose representative was turned down because the movie was about a different war. In the last hours before the opening, scalpers were demanding as much as $200 a ticket. Among those invited, apart from the governor and mayor and their entourages, were governors of seven other southern states; Herbert Hoover; Elsa Maxwell; Thomas Mann; the Billy Roses; the Averell Harrimans; an impressive roster of East Coast wealth including Jock Whitney, family groups of Whitneys and Vanderbilts, Nelson Rockefeller, J. P. Morgan and John Jacob Astor; and, of course, Margaret Mitchell.

The most notable absentees were Leslie Howard and Victor Fleming. Since the outbreak of war in Europe, Howard had been anxious to return to England; he left Hollywood at the end of August. Fleming had now been totally alienated by the advance publicity, in which Selznick was quoted as saying that all the directors on *Gone With the Wind* had been "supervised" by himself. The producer blamed this on the MGM publicity department, but Fleming declined even to discuss it. The breach between the two men became complete; this is one of the rare cases in which Selznick failed to heal a professional disagreement on the personal level. Not even Gable could persuade Fleming to go to Atlanta, nor to any of the other openings. The Hollywood celebrities traveled in separate planes. Selznick was accompanied by his wife, Myron, Vivien Leigh and Laurence Olivier, Olivia de Havilland; Gable and Carole Lombard joined a group of MGM executives on a plane with GONE WITH THE WIND painted in huge letters on the side of its fuselage. A deputation and a forty-piece band greeted both contingents as they arrived within a few minutes of each other at the airfield. The airfield, like the rest of the city, was festooned with flags and bunting. (Selznick had pleaded for a "secret" arrival, with Vivien and Gable first revealed in costume at a charity ball, but he was overruled.) A motorcade took them to the Georgian Terrace Hotel, streets and rooftops lined with people and the band playing "Dixie" over and over again. ("They're playing the song from the picture!" Vivien exclaimed. Fortunately none of the local journalists overheard.) At the hotel, the mayor officially greeted the stars and presented them with Wedgwood coffee and tea sets. That evening there was a charity ball on the Atlanta Bazaar set, transported from Hollywood, with the stars in costume, and the next day began with a luncheon with all the southern governors, followed by a tea party at the governor's mansion, followed by a cocktail party for the press, followed by the four-hour premiere itself.

The acclaim was everything for which Selznick could have hoped. When the applause and weeping from deeply affected southerners died down, general speech-making and congratulations occurred at the microphone. For the first time, Margaret Mitchell expressed a public opinion. She had warned Selznick that she would say nothing until this moment, and then it would be the truth. As overwhelmed as everyone else, she praised the producer's courage and determination and thanked him "on behalf of me and my poor Scarlett. . . . It's not up to me to speak of the grand things these actors have done, for they've spoken so much more eloquently than I could ever do." The day had been too exhausting for further official celebrations. After a long night's sleep the visitors gathered next day for a last function, a luncheon given by the author at the Riding Club. Then everyone went home.

Local reviews and the Hollywood trade papers were equally gratifying. Declining to analyze the picture's greatness, the *Motion Picture Herald* concluded: "One does not ask what Rembrandt's paints were made of, or what quarry furnished Angelo his stone." Straight to the point as usual, *Variety* called it "a great picture . . . poised for grosses which may be second to none in the history of the business."

Poised it was. Gala New York and Los Angeles openings followed, the latter attended by several unsuccessful contenders for the role of Scarlett: Paulette Goddard, Norma Shearer, and Joan Crawford. The Los Angeles event was marred for Selznick by Gable's attitude toward him. The star had now openly taken Fleming's side, and decided to let it be known. Their encounter was "strained and peculiar." But the New York reviews might have been written by MGM's publicity department. Frank Nugent in the *Times:* "The greatest motion picture mural we have seen and the most ambitious film-making venture in Hollywood's spectacular history." Archer Winsten in the *Post:* "Just as *Birth of a Nation* was a milestone of movie history, *Gone With the Wind* represents a supreme effort." At prices of 75¢ for matinees and $1 for evening performances (loges, $1.50), the picture began its extraordinary first run. At the end of it, in June 1940, over 25,000,000 people had paid admission.

Before this, at the Academy Award ceremonies on February 28, 1940, the industry had freighted Selznick with honors. *Gone With the Wind* won ten awards, more than any other picture before. Best picture; best actress, Vivien Leigh; best supporting actress, Hattie McDaniel (the first Oscar for a black performer, and the end of NAACP protests about the stereotyping of Negroes in the movie); best director, Victor Fleming, still angry and absent from the occasion; best screenplay, Sidney Howard; best photography, Ernest Haller and Ray Rennahan; a specially worded award to Cameron Menzies for his achievements in design and color; best art direction, Lyle Wheeler; best editing, Hal Kern and James Newcom; special effects, Jack Cosgrove; and the bonus of the Irving Thalberg Memorial Award "for the most consistent high level of production achievement by an individual producer" to Selznick himself. The neglect of Gable in favor of

Robert Donat in *Goodbye, Mr. Chips* acknowledged a big sentimental success; but Selznick, still regretting Gable's coolness toward him, was not too heady with triumph to complain. He reproached Russell Birdwell, convinced that the publicity campaign was somehow at fault. Later, and characteristically, he apologized.

Selznick had reached the climax of his career; it left him elated but uncertain. The screenwriter Frances Marion records in her autobiography, *Off With Their Heads!*, a chance meeting with him at the Ambassador Hotel in Los Angeles, soon after the awards. He was by himself, and said he'd like to buy her a drink and talk about his father. "There are times when I feel his hand on my shoulder. It wasn't there after we opened the picture in Atlanta, and I knew it was a success, but later, when I relaxed, confident of clear sailing ahead, that was when I felt him close." If he'd succeeded, it was because of Lewis J. Then he remembered that his father had often said, "No man can rest on his laurels," and began talking of his hopes for *Rebecca*. His mood seemed to alternate between pride and a need for reassurance. "Once you're on top you're in the position of a circus performer walking the high wire with no net underneath to catch you if you fall."

Presumably because she thought it was what he wanted to hear, Miss Marion assured Selznick that he would never fall, not with his father's hand on his shoulder.

eight

SPEAKING OF TARA

ECENTLY AN AMERICAN MOVIE captured popular imagination in a way that is being compared to the appeal of GWTW (as Selznick's film soon became known), but the comparison is misleading. Thirty years will have to pass before we can know if *The Godfather*'s appeal is momentary or lasting. In any case, unlike its predecessor, the involvement it demands never rises above the level of sensation, since its impact lies in showing the organization of violence, painstakingly detailed. Although made by a single director who also worked on the script, its style is strictly impersonal, the physical presentation craftsmanlike but without resonance or passion. *The Godfather* also differs from gangster movies of the '30s in never suggesting a world beyond its immediate world. Superficial though they were, *Scarface, G-Men,* and *Little Caesar* at least revealed something of the gangster's essence at the point of death or defeat; a kind of lonely disillusion overtook him as he realized the failure of his own particular line of private enterprise. In *The Godfather* the surface remains frozen; no one questions his own situation as a criminal, and the only issue is who gets the bullet first. The dead are simply those who can't think or shoot fast enough. The movie's success makes it obvious that acceptance of this idea is by no means limited to the Mafiosi. Assassinating a politician may cause a stir because the victim is famous, but the act of violence in itself is no longer surprising. When the most ruthless level of private enterprise becomes widely taken for granted, a film like *The Godfather* finds there are no questions left to be asked. Its characters exist in a nightmare which they (and the audience) accept as everyday reality.

GWTW comes from a time when questions were still being asked. The world it suggests beyond its immediate world is ambiguous. Scarlett may or may not get Rhett back — and if she doesn't, there is always Tara — but has she, at the age of twenty-eight, as Rhett asks her at the end (a line in the novel omitted from the movie), "gained the whole world and lost your own soul?" Again, are the horrors of the War responsible for her situation, or was it implicit in her character from the start? And when he leaves her, is Rhett the winner or the loser? In the final scene he also says — in a line rephrased from the novel — "I'm going back to Charleston, back where I belong. . . . I want to see if somewhere there isn't something left in life of charm and grace." He is seen, in fact, as retreating to the past, while Scarlett is left on her own in the present, like any individual coming to grips with a new world. Lucky because she escapes with her life, the possibility remains that she'll end up on a personal gallows. As with Rhett, it is uncertain whether she is a winner or a loser. At the end, nothing is truly certain — except that physical survival is not the only issue, and that a brutalized existence is something to be avoided. Life and the movies will coincide disturbingly, not for the first time, when in 1951 Vivien Leigh plays Blanche in the film of *A Streetcar Named Desire*. Eleven years later, Scarlett could easily have found herself drifting like

Tennessee Williams' lost lady, a similar victim of the myth of the old South as "a life of charm and grace."

Margaret Mitchell's novel spoke to so many readers because she was writing about a genuine dilemma. In spite of, or probably because of, the conventional romantic trappings, it struck a deep public nerve. Was there no choice, its vast audience of women asked themselves, between being a slave to men and circumstances, like Melanie, and ending up like Scarlett, independent but rejected? Setting the story in the past and making the characters southern, the author unconsciously strengthened her impact. The South is the only part of the American nation that has felt the reality of defeat, but in 1936, when the novel appeared, the whole nation had felt the possibility of it. This was the last act of the Depression. By the time the movie came out, the first act of World War II had opened in Europe, and the past seemed more violently alive than ever, since it mirrored so many uncertainties of the present.

The test of any work of art is its capacity for self-renewal. The most lasting ones seem to change and reveal further surprises with the passing of time. Although at moments the process work dates it technically, and its romanticism draws a few smiles now, GWTW passes this test on the basis of continuing emotional appeal, a familiar story constantly fascinating because of the vigor and intensity with which it is told. To theoreticians of any kind I realize that the idea of GWTW as a work of art on any level may be appalling. Most movie critics will only admit to the pantheon a work in which the director is the creator, and most other critics will find the material too simplified or bound by conventions. But the secret of American movie-making has always lain in creating something fresh from material not in itself particularly original. Like all popular art it is based on conventions, on genres — the western, the melodrama, the romantic comedy, the musical, the costume picture. Occasionally a personal artist transcends the genre — Hitchcock with melodrama, Chaplin and Lubitsch with comedy, Welles in *The Magnificent Ambersons* with the costume picture — and the outsider, the individual statement, breaks through; but for the most part American film-makers work within established rules and reflect popular preoccupations. The strength and the limitation of popular art is its close involvement with these moods; and obviously in looking at GWTW we should not expect a private or poetic approach to the past, as in the case of European directors like Ophuls or Renoir. We are looking at an archetype. From the other big American historical pictures, we remember moments and characters, like the battle charge and a few individual scenes in the otherwise fragmented *Birth of a Nation*, the chariot race in the otherwise ordinary *Ben Hur*; or we may be overwhelmed by the huge, absurd vulgarity, as in De Mille; but GWTW seems to me the only biggie that makes an experience in the past as a whole come alive.

It does this by sheer force and energy of presentation — the images and the people on the screen — which is the way all dramatic movies basically impose. Reading a novel, we think first and respond later; watching a movie, the process is reversed. In the novel of GWTW the issues are a little more thoroughly examined, and the characters of Rhett and Ashley have finer shadings; yet the loss of these elements seems minor when compared to the gain as a whole. As film-making, GWTW is superior to *Gone With the Wind* as novel-making.

The critical "problem" of GWTW as a movie without a real director is academic. Selznick was in that rare Hollywood situation, enjoyed by very few film-makers — Chaplin, Lubitsch, von Sternberg, Welles for a time and Stanley Kubrick today at a distance — who took or were given carte blanche. He differed from the others in being a producer instead of a director, not a producer in the sense of executive overseer, but someone who insisted that every creative element of a particular movie reflect his own personal choice. Even without the external pressures, I think he would have fired Cukor, or driven him to resign, because he didn't want any conflicting personal vision from a director who was an artist in his own right: the reverse of the usual battle when a director (as with Hitchcock and Selznick) is fighting the producer to make the film his own way.

In the end, all that counts is what is revealed on the screen, what Selznick called the personal signature. In GWTW it belongs to its producer, basically undiluted by any of his directors. His response to the material determined all the composite qualities on which a movie depends, structure, design, performances, rhythm, photography. It is useless to speculate on what might have happened if Cukor had finished the picture, for the simple reason that it *couldn't* have happened. Selznick was not willing to trust his property to anyone except an accountable delegate on the set, a technician who could show him, like a mirror image, the film already in his head. This underlying professional reality determined the situation; aggravating though it may be in its disregard of the rules, without Selznick there would have been no GWTW, and with him no other movie than the one which was made.

The main problem he had with Hitchcock on *Rebecca* was that Selznick couldn't understand his director's method of shooting — a "goddam jigsaw," as he called it. GWTW explains why, for its solid, direct, and detailed style reveals Selznick's schooling in the basic Hollywood techniques of the '30s, just as its classic antitheses of "success" and "happiness" are so firmly embedded in the same period. It is a mainstream style applied to a mainstream subject, using the medium to tell a chronologically assembled story, the camera a machine for seeing only as much as meets the eye. Freed from the theater, and unaware of what has happened in European movies, it looks instead to the nineteenth-century novel. Two years later, a much greater jigsaw puzzle than *Rebecca* was to confront Hollywood. Though disliked by most of the industry, *Citizen Kane* was to be imitated and borrowed from for years. Not, however, by Selznick, who even in decline clung to the methods of his youth, and found the tide increasingly against him. Before the revolution of *Kane*, before the far greater revolution of World War II, *GWTW* stands as his climax and valedictory.

From the opening, confidence sets the tone. "David O. Selznick has the Honor to Present," and then under the titles appear lusciously nostalgic shots of the old South — magnolias, sunsets, and contented darkies working in the fields. The first of several superimposed narrative titles, written by Ben Hecht but reworked by Selznick into the unmistakable style of his more oracular memos, tells us, "There was a land of Cavaliers and Cotton Fields called the Old South. . . . Look for it only in books, for it is no more than a dream remembered, a Civilization gone with the wind." The much re-shot first scene on the porch remains somewhat scrappy, curiously tentative after the rich musical overture and the credits: a script problem, basically, too much being attempted in too little time. Within less than two minutes Scarlett has to complain to the Tarleton twins, "Fiddle-de-dee! War, war, war! This war talk's spoiling the fun at every party!," tease them about whether they can take her to the Wilkes barbecue, then reveal simultaneously her love for Ashley and the stylistic convention whereby she will speak private thoughts aloud to the camera. The material on the screen is literally a patchwork, composed partly of Cukor's original scene and partly of retakes by Fleming and the director of special effects, Jack Cosgrove, shot by Lee Garmes and Ernest

Haller. Perhaps never in the history of the movies have so many hands been involved in so little footage.

With the arrival of Scarlett's father (Thomas Mitchell), the style becomes firmer. A beautiful shot as Mr. O'Hara gallops across the fields to meet Scarlett, the afternoon light hazy and dying; they walk up the hill together, and the camera performs the first of its long, impressive pull-backs — Tara at sunset, the sky a mass of drifting orange cloud, father and daughter silhouetted as they stand beside a tree with starkly twisted branches. On the sound track, Max Steiner's "Tara" theme swells proudly. As occasionally happens, the movie is poised here on the cliff of excess. But the shot is not held too long and the sunset *is* lovely, full-blown but not overblown.

The scale of the picture broadens at the Wilkes barbecue, after one of the few really obvious process shots in the film — a wobbly background plate of Twelve Oaks, sunlit and pillared, in front of which carriages draw up and guests stroll on the lawn. Inside, there are more guests, all exquisitely costumed, moving through the vast hallway and up the wide curved staircase. The introduction of Rhett is brilliantly managed. Scarlett first sees him standing at the foot of the staircase, a solitary figure in elegant black. He gives her a cool, challenging stare. She asks a girl-friend who the "nasty dark one" is, and turns away, not really interested in her reply. Color and texture are beautifully controlled in this sequence, the lighting subdued and airy, Rhett's black suit contrasted with the soft whites, greys and blues of the other costumes. It is one of the high points of Garmes's camera work in the picture. People dissolve in and out of shadow. Ashley and Melanie appear in silhouette as they move toward French windows, which Ashley opens to reveal a panorama of the lawn outside, the guests looking suddenly suspended in time; shutters filtering the light to a cool dusk, a Negro child fanning

the ladies stretched out for their afternoon siesta, stays loosened and hair down.

When Scarlett slips away from the others to find Ashley in the library and attack him with a declaration of love, she is on her way to the film's first intimate dramatic scene — which will reveal its only serious flaw. The role of Ashley is a difficult one, essentially weak and withdrawn but with an attractive facade; Leslie Howard seems unable to cut any kind of romantic figure, never the man at the touch of whose hand such a vibrant Scarlett trembles. I've already described Howard's embarrassed dislike of the part, and the problem of appearing in *Intermezzo* at the same time; even so, he seems barely concerned to hide his lack of involvement, and the attempt at a southern accent sounds amateur. In spite of Vivien Leigh's energy and passion, Scarlett's desire for him remains something we have to take on trust. Remote without being mysterious, the actor lowers the voltage in all their confrontations. Selznick and his editor must have been aware of his shortcomings, for the cutting always favors Scarlett in their scenes together.

The basic story, fortunately, is the duel of Scarlett and Rhett, and as they face each other for the first time — after it is revealed that Rhett has been lying hidden on a couch and has overheard Scarlett making love to Ashley — the voltage is high again. Scarlett may flounce out in anger and Rhett may pretend only to be amused, but left behind is a sharp sense of attraction underlying antagonism, of two people who will be unable to escape each other.

They meet again at the Atlanta Bazaar, Scarlett having recently become a widow. To spite Ashley, she has married Melanie's brother Charles, who is due to leave in a few days for the War but destined to die of measles before reaching any battle front. This time the outsider's figure in black is Scarlett in her widow's weeds, bored with pretending grief and surreptitiously jiggling her bustle to the music. As if to emphasize the gaiety around her, the colors are now festive, almost gaudy — Confederate flags in red and blue everywhere, bunting, banks of brilliant flowers, girls parading their party dresses. When Melanie takes off her wedding ring and offers it as a contribution to "The Cause," Rhett is genuinely impressed, for he knows her to be a great lady, very much in love with her husband; but when Scarlett, anxious to impress him and everyone else, offers *her* ring, all she gets from him is a lightly sarcastic, "I know how much that meant to *you*." But he shows his simultaneous desire and contempt for her when the ladies are asked to accept bids for themselves as dancing partners, again for "The Cause." As they take the floor at $10 a waltz, Rhett boldly calls out $150 for Scarlett. A sudden scandalized silence; Aunt Pittypat calls for her smelling salts. Undeterred, the widow steps into Rhett's arms. As they move off together, the camera shoots from a low angle, emphasizing the defiant whirls and billows of her black skirt.

Having crossed this barrier, and leveled with each other to some extent, Scarlett and Rhett ought to find themselves closer together. As usual with Scarlett and men, it goes wrong. Rhett made the offer as a challenge, never expecting her to accept it; now he realizes that she's more than a spoilt and fascinating girl, she has a kind of wild courage. But at the same time that she impresses him, he disappoints her. When she asks Rhett about his blockade running, which has made him a local hero, he answers that he's only in it for the money. Prepared to overlook his "vulgarity" if he's a patriot, Scarlett has no choice but to feel furious with him again.

In this scene, with its echoes of Fleming's work in *The Great Waltz*, we are given a hint of Scarlett's eventual personal defeat, just as we know the South will be defeated; and the camera effectively counterpoints both with its glimpses of the dancers, the decorations, the flags and defiant speech-making. A realist

in a superficial and selfish way, Scarlett at heart is still a romantic. Survival isn't going to be her problem — she's tough and resilient enough for that — but the blockage of her deeper feelings. She wants a hero and can't find one. She worships her father, but he becomes a drunkard and finally loses his mind. She adores Ashley, but her passion frightens him and he retreats to the safety of Melanie; she will continue to idealize him as a kind of gentleman-dreamer, not realizing his weakness and dishonesty until it's too late. And Rhett refuses to let her admire him. She mistakes his honesty for cynicism, and he becomes in her eyes "not a gentleman" — even though she cares no more about The Cause than he does. Worst of all, he has the bad manners to tell her that they're really alike, invading her life as the one reality that Scarlett, the self-professed realist, cannot accept.

The most original aspect of Vivien Leigh's performance is how she communicates this other side of Scarlett. Brilliant as her display of charm and willfulness is, she finds a great deal more in the role. The line that she insisted Selznick retain, in which she reflects that her mother brought her up to be kind and thoughtful and she's sorry to disappoint her, is in fact a key to the deeper level. For beyond the caprice and occasional cruelty of Scarlett is a lost innocence, a sense of childlike outrage that life has not turned out the way she had been promised it would.

Throughout the first half, the story of Scarlett and Rhett is told against a background of the South in disintegration. Like all the elements in the picture, foreground and background are very skillfully blended. Cameron Menzies' remarkable exterior set of Atlanta emerges piece by piece, used only as the action demands; no panoramic shot to advertise a vast and massive reconstruction, just details of a world that in its turn will go up in smoke. This is also a movie about the Civil War without any extensive battle scenes, its evocation of the War itself limited to a few spectacular shots of wounded and dead Confederate soldiers at the railroad depot and in the countryside, and glimpses of ragged soldiers during the retreat from Atlanta. The sense of impending collapse is conveyed most vividly off-screen, in a brief exchange between Ashley and Scarlett when he explains that from what he's seen, he knows the South is lost. "Some of our men are barefooted now," he says in a line written by Fitzgerald, "and the snow is deep in Virginia." For the rest, we see the War as something that people go off to, and may or may not come back from; casualty lists are passed around in the square outside the newspaper office.

The War becomes a direct threat for the first time when Scarlett, leaving the hospital where she grudgingly does volunteer work as a nurse, walks out to the street and hears the sound of shells exploding as the bombardment begins. Suddenly the street is filled with panic-stricken people, horses rear up, dust and smoke billow across. In a masterly series of shots, the camera follows Scarlett, concentrating on her reactions. (This sequence was directed by Cameron Menzies.) Characteristically, she never seems really afraid, only distracted and impatient, then relieved when Rhett appears in a buggy and takes her home to Aunt Pittypat. It's as if the camera reflects Scarlett's own narrow, restricted view of the situation, for when Rhett tells her that Atlanta is doomed and she must get out, she refuses at first to believe him.

The understated camera style seems to have built up to this point. Until the city actually burns, Scarlett's part in the War is incidental, her only important concern that Ashley's name should not turn up on a casualty list. A constant use of shadows suggests how shadowy everything outside her own life appears to her. In a brief sequence (Cameron Menzies again) showing Scarlett and Melanie at work in the hospital, their figures are seen first as dim, elongated silhouettes thrown against a wall, and at the end of it the camera moves back to them. When the city starts to burn, Scarlett is helping to deliver Melanie's baby at Aunt Pittypat's house, and again the two women — and the baby, when we see it — are silhouettes in a blurred twilit room. One of the few Cukor scenes preserved intact, beautifully photographed by Garmes, it has a subtle texture and a strange, jittery atmosphere — Scarlett in a sudden fury slapping the frightened black servant, Prissy. Earlier, when Scarlett has tried to find a doctor for Melanie, an extraordinarily vivid point has been made. She walks into the city, the camera again following closely; then, as she approaches the railroad depot, the camera

pulls back slowly to its famous crane shot of the wounded and dying Confederate soldiers. Scarlett finds Doctor Meade tending one of them, and he's amazed when she asks him to come and help her deliver Melanie's baby. "Are you crazy? I can't leave these men for a baby! They're dying — hundreds of them!" His reaction bewilders her — and we realize that Scarlett hasn't really seen what the camera has seen.

The viewpoints finally coincide during the escape from Atlanta. Sitting beside Rhett in the wagon, Scarlett sees a huge wall of fire. As they pass it, a building collapses in flames. They reach the freightyards and see a box car loaded with explosives. Sparks and embers from another nearby building are falling on it, and the car starts to explode as Rhett and Scarlett disappear behind a dense, billowing cloud of smoke. (The matching here of the process work with the master shots of the fire as originally filmed is technically remarkable.) When we see Rhett and Scarlett again, they're on a road at the edge of the city. The sky is an angry, overpowering red. They pass remnants of Confederate troops, exhausted and bedraggled. A young soldier sways on his feet and drops to the ground as the wagon passes. Seeing all this, facing the reality of the War for the first time, Scarlett is not too shaken to be indignant. "They make me sick," she exclaims, "all of them! Getting us all into this with their swaggering and boasting." At the time, this was no doubt intended to show the hard, selfish side of Scarlett; viewed today, from the other side of World War II, Korea, and Vietnam, it seems one of her most sympathetic moments, the impatience wholly appealing and the lack of pity supremely healthy.

A curious and original scene follows. Having rescued Scarlett, Rhett now proposes to abandon her. He stops the wagon in open country, hands her the reins. She can't believe it. "You should *die* of shame to leave me here alone and helpless!" He tells her,

"Heaven help the Yankees if they capture *you*," and confides a sudden attack of patriotism. "I'm going to join up with our brave lads in grey." Scarlett again doesn't believe it, but can't understand why he jokes at a time like this. Amused, Rhett insists that he's serious, and reminds her that southerners can never turn down a losing cause. He demands a goodbye kiss, wanting Scarlett to play the scene of a soldier's sweetheart bidding him farewell. He puts his arms around her, and now it's only in part a charade. If she yields, he'll stay — but she doesn't, because this is a farewell scene she's already played in her mind with Ashley, and the memory of it makes her furious again. She slaps Rhett violently in the face. (Scarlett's slaps always mean business.) Still amused, he hands her his dueling pistol and disappears into the darkness.

Rhett's behavior in this scene offers a glimpse of his personal nihilism that Scarlett simply doesn't see, as she never saw the wounded soldiers at the railroad depot. All she understands is a vulgar and outrageous proposal. Once again they have come together and found themselves antagonists. In Scarlett's eyes, Rhett has rescued her and ought to behave like a hero. Instead, his joking conceals a soundly realistic proposal — the world is going to pieces around them, and they should run away together. But this is not the proposal of a hero or a gentleman; it leaves Scarlett confused and resentful, and it never occurs to her that if she refuses him, Rhett will in fact go off to join his lost cause.

The journey back to Tara with Prissy, Melanie, and the baby becomes her first major endurance test. She is completely on her own, making her way through a no-man's-land occasionally crossed by the enemy. These sequences, conceived and directed by Cameron Menzies, have practically no dialogue and a sustained visual power. A bridge over a river at night, during a rainstorm: Union soldiers pass overhead, while underneath Scarlett huddles in the wagon that she's driven into the water. In brilliant daylight, vultures hover above a deserted battlefield strewn with dead. Night again when Scarlett reaches Twelve Oaks, and finds it looted and burned. Inside, the hallway and staircase we saw at the barbecue are gutted. As the journey continues, and they approach Tara, she becomes panic-stricken; then the moon, emerging from behind a cloud, shows the house still there, silent and ghostly but untouched. She is met in the hallway by a troubled Mammy and her father with a haunted look on his face. Opening a door, she discovers her dead mother, fully clothed with a still, waxen face, laid out on a table in a room. (This shot is deliberately echoed later on, when Rhett stares at the dead body of his and Scarlett's child, Bonnie Blue.) Scarlett's reaction is memorably handled here. She doesn't move, only utters a loud, wild scream, and the quick fade-out suggests that an innermost cord has been cut. Scarlett derives much of her strength from Mrs. O'Hara, a lady with a gentle manner and an iron will. Losing her, Mr. O'Hara declines quickly into alcoholism and feeble-mindedness. Scarlett's curious tenderness with his state throws into relief her passion for Ashley — she is drawn to weak men, of which there is no shortage in this society of remarkably strong women. All her later difficulties with Rhett will stem from resentment of his strength. Circumstances now force her to become, as she says, "the head of the house," and it turns into a role she finds impossible to give up.

Part One ends with Scarlett's defiant declaration of rights. Wandering exhausted and hungry through the fields, she plucks the radish from the earth, tries to eat it and retches. "As God is my witness," she tells the camera, "they're not going to lick me. . . . I'm going to live through this and when it's over I'll never be hungry again. No, nor any of my folks! If I have to lie — steal — cheat — kill — as God is my witness, I'll never be hungry again." The camera pulls back again, and Steiner's music swells up again, until she becomes a heroic silhouette, standing

on Margaret Mitchell's "savagely red land," in the violent light of dawn. This famous moment now seems rather crudely theatrical. The film becomes poster art, Scarlett a billboard figure representing Survival — though it might have been saved but for the "Tara" theme on ambrosial strings, hardly appropriate to a climax of anger and desolation.

In Part Two the tone is immediately more bleak and sardonic, as we see a life at Tara totally stripped of its antebellum ease and charm. "In the days that followed, Tara might have been Crusoe's desert island, so still it was, so isolated from the rest of the world." Raggedly dressed, Scarlett's two sisters are picking withered-looking cotton in stark and blackened fields; Scarlett is drawing water from a well; Mr. O'Hara leans against a fence in a private, loony world of his own. "Mother said you could always tell a lady by her hands," Suellen complains, mortified by her calluses, then turns on Scarlett — "I hate Tara!" She receives another of her sister's ferocious slaps, and the two girls go back to work, stifling their tears.

Returning to the house, Scarlett is confronted by a Union deserter intent on loot and, probably, rape. This is another Cukor scene, handled with a fine tension and containing an extraordinary close-up of Scarlett right after she shoots the soldier with Rhett's pistol, her face sullen and ravaged with shock. The episode also shows Melanie in a new and more amusing light. Hearing the shot, she comes out of her bedroom in a nightgown, still obviously weak, sees the body at the foot of the stairs and gently, pitilessly takes murder in her stride. "Do you think it would be dishonest if we went through his haversack?" Scarlett glances at her for once with genuine respect. "I'm ashamed I didn't think of it myself."

When they find he was carrying a few gold pieces, the prospect of immediate famine recedes. Shortly after this comes the news that the War is over, and Scarlett's reaction — in contrast to the spontaneous rejoicing of the others — suggests the change occurring in her. "We'll plant more cotton. Cotton ought to go sky high next year." Ashley returns, the only person who could affect this change. When she begs him to run away with her, she has a sudden insight into her own predicament and is really begging him to save her from herself, from what she fears she's going to become. "I do want to escape, too! I'm so very tired of it all!" But of course he talks about Melanie and honor, and the door closes. As I mentioned earlier, the scene was played with greater intensity in the test, but in Fleming's version there is a fine, terse moment when Scarlett turns away, realizing she's lost,

Lining up for a shot of Scarlett searching for Rhett in Atlanta after the war.

and summons a tired and wintry composure. "It won't happen again," she says flatly, and walks back to the house.

From now on she will bury her personal life and concentrate on saving Tara. Needing more money to pay the taxes, she is coolly prepared to sell herself to Rhett, but unfortunately he's not able to buy. (After a few insane months in the Confederate army, he went back to blockade-running, banked the proceeds in England, and was jailed as a war profiteer.) Walking disconsolately through the streets of Atlanta — a sequence containing some vivid glimpses of the beginnings of Reconstruction — she becomes more lively when she encounters Suellen's beau, the weak and trusting Frank Kennedy. She tricks and charms him into marrying her, then proceeds to take over his modestly successful lumber business. More than that, she persuades Ashley to work for her, and in doing so destroys his last vestige of self-respect. Reducing both her unloved husband and the lover who won't have her to employees, Scarlett embarks on the life of a lady tycoon and discovers the frigid consolations of money. She develops into an excellent businesswoman, greedily prepared to exploit the pathetic cheap labor available. And as she sublimates her private feelings into power, the two men secretly sublimate their loss of power into violence.

Up to this point, the dramatic line of Part Two is clearly sustained. Now, due to some shaky condensations in the script, it stumbles. In the novel, Ashley and Frank Kennedy join the Klan; in the movie, Frank meets his death when, with Ashley and others, he goes to clean up Shanty Town after a Negro has attacked Scarlett there. Selznick removed all references to the Klan because he didn't want to offend southern audiences or to lose sympathy for Ashley, but the problem of dramatizing how this most unviolent man turns to violence is unresolved. There is no scene in which Leslie Howard can express Ashley's bitterness and perplexity, his shame in being a partner to Scarlett's exploitations, the man that Margaret Mitchell describes at this point as "gnawed by a scarcely endurable pain." As a result, the episode with Scarlett, Melanie, and the other women waiting for their husbands to return from the raid occurs without preparation.

"*Tension,*" the screenplay instructs in one of its rare laconic moments, and evidently there had been tension in getting the scene ready. It was a section of the script that Sidney Howard had been brought out to rewrite. "We first read that scene a day or so in advance of the shooting," de Havilland told me, "in the set, with all its props. David wanted Sidney Howard to be present

then. . . . Sidney, at David's request, actually read the scene aloud to us before we rehearsed it." On the screen, there is still not enough beneath the surface for the actors to play; and the director, Sam Wood, goes for big close-ups of a ticking clock, anxious faces, the ladies' hands at their sewing — a textbook approach that was probably unavoidable. Later, when the men return and Melanie discovers from Rhett what has happened, there is a revealing moment, brilliantly seized by the actress, as she rises sweetly but invincibly to the occasion, echoing her reaction to the deserter shot by Scarlett. That Ashley has been involved in a killing gives her no pause; she's concerned only to protect him from suspicion. Once again, de Havilland has a crucial memory of "going to see George at his house on a Sunday afternoon, to ask him his views about this scene and how he thought Melanie should react in it."

As a whole the longest and least skillful cuts in the novel have been made here. Margaret Mitchell took one hundred and fifty pages to get from Frank Kennedy's marriage to his death; the screenplay takes twenty-five. Much of the original is disposable, but it seems that in his impatience to reach the central story of Scarlett and Rhett again, Selznick sacrificed momentum to pace. It was Sam Wood's bad luck to be assigned most of these scenes (and may account for his being untypically "testy" during the shooting, in Lydia Schiller's remembering); his work is solidly competent, and even a highly imaginative director would have found it difficult to disguise their fragmented nature. Selznick was editing and rewriting the script daily at this point, and the pressure shows.

Ashley is not the only one skimped in the script, because the toll that Scarlett exacts from herself in her obsession with security is also underdramatized. In the novel, she visits her grandmother after the War and explains how she felt when she got back to Tara and found her mother dead. "On the way home I thought the worst had already happened to me, but when I knew she was dead I knew what the worst really was." The grand-mother says, "It's a very bad thing for a woman to face the worst that can happen to her, because after she's faced the worst she can't ever really fear anything again." In losing this scene, or an equivalent, what is also lost is the ironic point that Scarlett, after all, is still afraid. The ruthless marriage with Frank and the emergence of Scarlett as super-businesswoman are really acts of brilliantly camouflaged fear; but the movie stops short of conveying the desperation behind them, and Scarlett herself becomes for a while merely hard and one-dimensional. Her use-less attempt at seducing Rhett before she discovers he's tem-porarily out of money, and her shrewd appraisal of Kennedy's situation are entertainingly done — but the consequences are missing. At this point in her life Scarlett is not just an ingenious schemer; she is discovering the bitterness of self-reliance.

With Rhett's proposal to Scarlett, momentum is recovered. Knowing her well enough by now to realize his only chance of winning her is by disguising his real feelings, he turns it into a romantic charade. Going down on his knees, he declares, "It cannot have escaped your notice that for some time past the friendship I have felt for you has ripened into a deeper feeling. A feeling more beautiful, more pure, more sacred. . . . Dare I name it? Can it be — love?" This time it works. Scarlett is drunk and depressed anyway, bored with the role of female tycoon; Rhett has spoken all those words remembered from her earlier innocence, "beautiful," "pure," "sacred," and she not only lets him make love to her but finds herself responding with unguarded passion. It is one of the best scenes in the whole movie — the tension underlying Rhett's bravado, Scarlett's deliciously imprac-tical attempts to disguise the fact that she's been at the bottle, her longing to escape from herself — unerringly staged by Flem-

ing and elegantly photographed, with shutters filtering the light in Aunt Pittypat's parlor to create a falsely romantic atmosphere.

The rest of the movie is mainly concerned with the marriage of Rhett and Scarlett, the approach to it a curious and effective mixture of muted Strindberg and popular convention. Just as Rhett is careful never to expose his deeper feelings, so Scarlett never makes up her mind (until it's too late) what her feelings are. Even on the honeymoon — another sequence directed by Fleming with strong kinetic flair, swiftly evoking Scarlett's new world of pleasure, the riverboat in the moonlight, the gaudy cancan dancers at the New Orleans restaurant — the novelty of being a sex object, pampered with new clothes and jewels, doesn't entirely satisfy her. Lying back in the riverboat cabin, she suddenly smiles. "I'm thinking about how rich we are. Rhett — I can keep the lumber business too, can't I?" Rhett hopes that by giving her everything she asks for (a new house, the restoration of Tara), she'll capitulate in the end and admit that she truly loves him. But as soon as the honeymoon is over, restlessness starts to gnaw at Scarlett; she begins to feel she has sold herself. Still haunted by what Rhett has said to her earlier — "We're alike. . . . Selfish and shrewd, but able to look things in the eyes and call them by their right names." — she recognizes its truth, finds it humiliating and very unromantic. When she cuts off sexual relations with Rhett after the birth of their daughter, it is to try and convince herself that she's really superior to him, and to find a way of striking back.

Here a brief but vital scene from the novel is omitted, and the effect is to reduce Scarlett. In the movie she bars Rhett from her bedroom because her waist has thickened since the birth of the baby, and she never wants to have another child. In the novel, while Scarlett is extremely cross at what motherhood has done to her figure, it is Ashley who brings about the decision. He tells her that Rhett is beginning to "brutalize" her — "I've

got to say it, your Rhett Butler, everything he touches is poison."
In true mealy-mouthed Ashley fashion he then offers a gentle-
manly apology. "No one has a right to criticize a husband to a
wife" — but the poison has now entered Scarlett's mind. Going
home, she decides that Ashley is jealous of Rhett, which means
that he still really loves her. She will "keep" herself for Ashley
by denying herself to Rhett. Without this, Scarlett's action in
the movie seems too petty, typical of the kind of thing Vivien
Leigh complained about when she was afraid that Scarlett would
emerge as just a shallow bitch. At one moment during the scene
with Rhett one can see the actress trying to convey motives lacking in the dialogue. When Rhett lays his hands on her shoulders,
she turns away with a violent, almost frightening revulsion. The
gesture is so original that it disconcerts, then one realizes that
she has briefly found a deeper layer in the situation.

Otherwise the stages of the duel are vividly shown. Fleming is
again at his best in the famous scene when Scarlett comes down-
stairs in the middle of the night to find Rhett drinking by himself in the diningroom — a beautiful movement by the camera
as it edges around the half-open double doors, disclosing first
the long, oppressive, candlelit room, and then Rhett slumped on
a chair at the long table. Lonely and angry, he alternates between
appeal and threat, then suddenly loses patience, picks Scarlett up
and carries her protestingly upstairs. At the time she is furious,
but next morning it's clear she enjoyed the experience. (Vivien
Leigh once said that what Scarlett needed was "a good old-
fashioned spanking," but this scene suggests that a good old-
fashioned lay was more important.) When Rhett comes into her
bedroom next morning, she's ready for a complete reconcilia-
tion — but in another reversal, reminiscent of the moment
when he abandons her outside Atlanta, he behaves as if it never
happened and announces he is going off on a trip.

Today, of course, these scenes would be sexually franker, but not necessarily stronger. In the conflict between Scarlett and Rhett, sex is only one weapon. Theirs is essentially a clash between two fiercely independent but frustrated people, Rhett intent on possession and Scarlett determined to resist it. As Fitzgerald noted, the material is not in itself "original" — but no other American film has presented it through such larger-than-life figures, made even larger and more heroic by classic star performances. Apart from the contrived, soap-opera twist of the death of Bonnie Blue, there is no schmaltz, only the broad romantic strokes that a legend demands. Gable, particularly, has great impact in these scenes. His personal temperament, the vulnerability beneath masculine assurance, is an enormous natural advantage; but he also conveys strikingly the predicament of Rhett — loving Scarlett but knowing that if he ever betrays the depth of his feelings he's lost; finding some consolation with the kind-hearted whore, Belle Watling, yet still trapped in his old-fashioned notion of a "good" wife, spoiled and adoring. It can never be gratified, because the wife he wants has closed herself off. These are situations deeply woven into the fabric of American life.

Melanie's death finally frees Scarlett, too late and in a way she hadn't expected. Coming out of the bedroom, she finds Ashley distractedly clutching one of his dead wife's gloves. "I don't know where the mate to this is — she must have put it away." When she sees him broken and helpless, hears him admit that without Melanie he is nothing, Scarlett at last realizes how much of her life she has wasted on a fantasy. "I've loved something that doesn't really exist," she says, half to herself, then runs out of the house, hurrying back through the fog to find Rhett. She returns to a house that seems chillingly empty, calls his name and gets no answer. She discovers him upstairs, sitting morosely in a chair in his bedroom, bags already packed. Exhausted by their years of struggle, all he wants now is to escape from the pain it's caused him. Scarlett tells him that she's finally ready to face her own feelings — "I must have loved you for years, only I'm such a stupid fool I didn't know it" — but he can only reply, "That's your misfortune." Now that her obsession with Ashley has gone, he finds his own desire for her has gone as well. Too old to believe in sentimentalities like starting all over again, he delivers his last, rueful line, and goes out of the door. Scarlett is left staring after a second lost, unrealizable passion, reflecting that "had she ever understood Ashley, she would never have loved him; had she ever understood Rhett, she would never have lost him."

For a moment she looks crestfallen, then the old energy and determination return. The voices of her father, Rhett, and Ashley remind her of her strength and its source, Tara, and then for the last time she addresses the camera: "I'll go home — and I'll think of some way to get him back. After all, tomorrow is another day!" A slow dissolve from the close-up of her tear-stained, little-girl's face to a long shot of the earlier, hardened Scarlett in the fields at dawn, heroic silhouette once more as the camera pulls back for the last time from this symbol of the South that would never admit defeat even, as the author rather ominously comments, "when it stared them in the face."

Selznick's insistence on an intermission between the two parts of GWTW was justified not only by physical necessities, but by the need of a pause to prepare the audience for an emotional shift. The structural lapses in Part Two, due to some lack of skill in telescoping a mass of events in a long work, are probably responsible for the majority opinion that it is inferior to the first half. The same problem occurred with the movie of *David Copperfield*; when reproached that its second half was less consistently gripping than the first, Cukor answered that the same was true of the novel. In both movies the same decision was taken, to follow the strengths and weaknesses of the original, and when the original is so overwhelmingly familiar and popular, it seems unavoidable. In one way *Gone With the Wind* has the edge on *David Copperfield*, whose hero grows up into a rather uninteresting young man; but if you respond to Rhett and Scarlett, then the second half of *GWTW* will seem only incidentally unsatisfactory, for it contains their strongest and most revealing moments. Less of a whole than Part One, it rises to individually more powerful episodes. Even if the script problems had been completely resolved, the movie would still have inherited the novel's narrowing-down structure, from the panoramic approach of Part One to the more enclosed personal dramas of Part Two.

Much has also been made of the difference in visual style between the two sections. Although the texture of Part Two is generally less subtle, the truth is that most of its scenes offer fewer opportunities for variations in tone. Ranging from nostalgic evocation of the old South to the confusion and panic of war, Part One makes much greater demands; Part Two, restricted in scope and with less physical movement, becomes less rich on this account, not because of the change in cameramen. Without hindsight, it would be impossible to detect that two scenes in Aunt Pittypat's house — the birth of Melanie's baby in Part One, and Rhett's proposal to Scarlett in Part Two — were created by different directors and cameramen. Their texture is remarkably similar. The same is true of the sequences of Scarlett in the streets of Atlanta during the bombardment, and at the beginning of Reconstruction. The only scenes that strike me as visually uncertain in Part Two are those in the house that Rhett builds for Scarlett. Its exterior, though detectably a process shot, is a charming gingerbread confection; its interiors are confused, and here Selznick, probably through his art director and cameraman, is at fault. In the novel, Margaret Mitchell makes it clear that the house reflects Scarlett's taste, which Rhett at one moment wryly compares to Belle Watling's. In the movie we don't know whose taste is reflected by the stained-glass window at the top of the stairs, the general excess of plush and ornamentation. Unlike the houses in *The Magnificent Ambersons* or *Gaslight*, it neither comments on a life-style of the time nor provides a really dramatic frame for the action. Lee Garmes has said that Selznick later regretted firing him; his loss is principally felt here, for his more sophisticated eye could have made the point, emphasizing the whorehouse quality of Scarlett's wealth through a beaded lamp, a piece of statuary, a pretentious chandelier. On the other hand, this point is probably beyond Selznick's intention. He seems just to have wanted an ornately impressive set.

Otherwise Part Two contains some strongly atmospheric images, the mournful, rundown look of Tara after the War, the glimpses of Atlanta during Reconstruction, Shanty Town with its squalid tents and lean-tos, Aunt Pittypat's stuffy little parlor; and the unifying visual touch certainly comes from Cameron Menzies. Also, a breath of fresh air literally transforms the long dolly shot in which Scarlett and Rhett, out walking with their daughter, exchange social pleasantries with unseen neighbors as they pass by. Filmed on an exterior set during a windy day, the sequence gains additional wit through Scarlett almost losing her hat as she tries to create an impression of domestic bliss with a dutifully gracious smile.

Like "Rosebud" in *Citizen Kane*, Tara is a symbolic key to the central character — but a practical one as well. The child's sled, disappearing into flames at the end, may be a reminder of lost innocence; but Tara continues to exist, a place to go back to. In its very different way, Welles's movie is concerned with the same thing: the life of someone dedicated to material success and self-sufficiency at the expense of "love." The highly personal and the highly popular work of art emerge from the same pre-occupation. Kane, of course, is a much more complex and impressive figure than Scarlett, his ambition more overwhelming — he wants fame and power as well as riches — but both stories at the end raise the same question: "Was it worth it?" The answer in *Kane* is far less agreeable, for the movie leaves behind a sense of desolation and wrecked lives, and has shown us the mean, lonely old age of its protagonist, whereas Scarlett is left youthful and energetic, the havoc she's caused fairly modest in comparison.

Kane is an exceptional, mysterious being; he has a fearful and remote aura that Scarlett lacks. (This is why she remains an infinitely more popular figure.) The things that happen to Scarlett seem exceptional at the time because she *feels* them to be so, and the movie conveys her feeling; but if we examine the events of her life, she does nothing truly controversial or devastating. Misled by a weak man who uses noble phrases, she condemns herself to a dream lover and botches her chances of personal happiness. The obsession causes her to marry one man out of revenge, a second for money, and a third out of desperation. The only person on whom she inflicts real unhappiness is Rhett, who knew the score from the start. Along the way she discovers that at times of crisis she can be totally self-sufficient, and no matter what happens, she can take it. This strength is often admirable, for it saves the lives of Melanie and her baby; it only becomes an insoluble problem with Rhett, whom she cannot understand until she's driven him out the door. Badly though she treats him at times, it is nothing in comparison with what Strindberg's couples do to each other, or what Gudrun does to Gerald in *Women in Love*. All of which, again, explains her hold on popular imagination. The waters in which she finds herself are not too deep to scare off wide identification, and thousands of women would have enjoyed the risk of getting into them, just as thousands of men would have liked to walk out on their wives in the manner of Rhett.

Not long after he finished the first draft of GWTW, Sidney Howard compared the producer of movies to the New Zealand kiwi bird, which has wings but is unable to fly. Perhaps he intended this to explain why Selznick drew back from assuming the full responsibility of writing and directing the picture. Having initiated it, worked with writers, rewritten their work, chosen the cast, and fired the first director, the logical step would have been to take over completely on the set. There are other producers with a similar history of overseeing their films in exhausting detail, pressuring and depleting their directors, and again stopping short. The answer must be that Selznick, like the others, was at once jealous and afraid of the director's role, seeing it as a mystery he didn't care to confront. He was technically very knowledgeable, and he insisted on creative authority, yet he continually pursued artist-directors — Cukor, Hitchcock, de Sica, Huston — and finally quarreled with all of them. Obviously he felt more secure with first-rate and resourceful craftsmen like Fleming, Wellman, and Charles Vidor, who could never threaten him on the creative level. Wanting "art" and increasingly unwilling to grant an artist-director autonomy: this was a conflict that Selznick never resolved.

James Agee once described the Selznick style as "lively but aesthetically self-defeating, peculiar yet imitable," which seems to me true of the later films, but not of the earlier ones. *Little Women* and *Duel in the Sun* have no style in common. The first displays a light, graceful romanticism that is unmistakably Cukor's; the second is orgiastic *kitsch* in the manner favored by King Vidor in his later years, but blown up by Selznick to proportions undreamed of even by the director of *The Fountainhead*. Again, though the material of *Rebecca* is perhaps more Selznick than

Hitchcock, the director managed to transform it into a personal work. But GWTW represents the summit of what can be called the Selznick style, a once-in-a-lifetime confrontation of method and material. (A major problem of Selznick's later years was that he never again found material half as good.) Beyond this, what GWTW lacks in personal manner it makes up for in personal conviction. Dominating his remarkable army of artists and technicians, Selznick brought off the supreme Hollywood custom-built movie — on which, because of its subject, reality has conferred a lasting relevance. Unless the world changes unforeseeably, the experience with which it deals can never date. During World War II both novel and film were banned in Nazi-occupied Europe by Goebbels, who saw the story of people resisting defeat as potentially subversive. When the movie opened in the liberated cities of Europe in 1945, public response was almost delirious. De Havilland, the picture's only surviving star, has described its effect in Paris: the French saw it as "a story about surviving a defeat; physical survival at any price, as you see it in Scarlett; and the kind of spiritual survival represented by Melanie — the endurance of a system of values from a civilization that has been wiped out." On other countries, in the same dismal aftermath, the impact was equal. In Amsterdam and Vienna they wept like southerners after the premiere in Atlanta.

This continuing appeal emphasizes how the movie's lack of historical analysis works in its favor. It is no more concerned with the reasons behind the Civil War than with the situation of Negroes in the antebellum South. The War is seen merely as a kind of unforgivable personal affront to Scarlett, which is the way thousands of younger people over the world look at any war today. The Negro types, as in the novel, unquestioningly reflect the time in which it takes place. (Hattie McDaniel's splendid Mammy, by the way, is far less of a caricature than

Laura Hope Crews's Aunt Pittypat.) Such perfect enclosure within its period only increases the movie's force as a legend. Seeing the film again in the '70s, one finds no shadows of polemic to obscure the fascination of watching personal history repeat itself.

There remains a shadow of a different kind, a technical point. In 1967, two years after Selznick's death, MGM released GWTW for the seventh time, but not in its original form. For the big-screen era, the company decided to enlarge its 35mm negative to 70mm, and add stereophonic sound. This involved a frame-by-frame reprocessing, which had a variable effect on the color; in brighter scenes, such as the Atlanta Bazaar, little harm is done, but there are many others from which the subtlety and richness have been drained. The current prints give an incomplete idea of the movie's visual sophistication, and even more damaging is the projection on a wider screen. The compositions appear frequently distorted or out-of-rack. Selznick once estimated that his deal with MGM for the services of Gable cost him a personal profit of $25,000,000. One wonders, had he lived to see it, how he would estimate the cost of his reputation by the way his film is now projected.

nine

AFTERLIVES

A T THE TIME OF GWTW's premiere in Atlanta, David
Selznick was thirty-seven years old. Since his arrival in
Hollywood in 1926 he had produced more than fifty
films. During the remaining twenty-five years of his
life, after GWTW, he produced nine. The record, as they say,
speaks for itself.

Between *Rebecca*, which came out in 1940, and *Since You
Went Away*, there was a gap of four years; it would seem that
Lewis J. Selznick's hand continued to rest on his son's shoulder,
for the time was taken up almost exclusively with financial ma-
neuvers. By April 1942, GWTW had been re-released twice,
and the profits enabled David to pay off Selznick International's
bank debt of around $3,000,000. There remained a personal
profit of over $2,000,000, which he decided to convert from
highly taxable personal income to capital gains, by selling his interest in the picture to Jock Whitney and dissolving their company. In order to increase this profit, he came to an arrangement
with MGM whereby various overheads were added to the
movie's original budget; after this time, he always estimated the
cost of GWTW at $4,250,000. In turn, Whitney sold out his

interest in *GWTW* to MGM in 1944, reserving only the television rights, for which another deal was made several years later. Thus MGM became the sole owner of the theatrical rights to the picture after its second re-run, reaping all the profits of five more major re-releases.

Other valuable assets remained the property of David's new company, David Selznick Productions, which he formed after dissolving the partnership with Whitney. They included a number of talented people under contract — Hitchcock, Vivien Leigh, Ingrid Bergman, Joan Fontaine, Gregory Peck, Joseph Cotten, Dorothy McGuire — all of whom made more pictures for other companies than for Selznick. He loaned them out at considerable profit to himself and also developed "packages" — *Jane Eyre* with John Houseman as producer, Fontaine as star, Robert Stevenson as director; Hitchcock's *Saboteur* and *Notorious* — but instead of producing them, he sold them to the highest bidder. In the case of *Saboteur* this was very damaging for Hitchcock. Universal paid so much for the package that it had to impose visible economies on the actual production.

During these years of the Selznick empire, David also decided to form his own releasing organization — a curiously abstract extravagance, since it involved setting up nationwide offices to handle an absence of movies. The Selznick Releasing Organization was constantly promised products that never materialized. As well as the packages, David acquired the rights to a number of best-selling novels and successful Broadway plays, among them *The Keys of the Kingdom*, *Waterloo Bridge*, and *Claudia*; but once again he sold them to other companies for the same hijacker's ransom. Another manipulation seemed as abstract as the releasing company, but in the end he made money out of it. Continuing his habit of listing literary classics that he might one day want to film, Selznick placed them on what was known as the "reserved" list. Within the industry there existed a gentleman's agreement (convenience, not irony, is implied in the use of this phrase): once a novel or play in public domain was registered on this list, it could not be filmed by anyone else for three years. Among Selznick's titles were seven plays by Shakespeare. He made no attempt to realize a film from any of them, but when John Houseman came to produce *Julius Caesar* at MGM it was discovered that Selznick still "owned" it. His price for relinquishing the title was that MGM should buy the rights to two literary properties he'd recently acquired — again, of course, without any intention of producing them.

At the time of *Jane Eyre* — and of *Saboteur*, on which he also worked with Hitchcock — Houseman had been under the impression that Selznick wanted him to produce films under the company's sponsorship while its president "rested on his laurels and watched the money roll in." After these experiences he realized that Selznick "had not the slightest intention of letting anyone produce pictures at his studio except himself." And not even, during these years, himself. He amassed considerable resources — a studio, contract players and directors, properties, distribution offices — without using any of them. His world had reached the edge of change, and creatively he seemed paralyzed. With the erosion of foreign markets due to World War II, economy became the watchword at the studios, and this in itself must have seemed distasteful. Lower budgets and the arrival of refugee directors from Europe encouraged the flowering of a modest new popular genre, the "black" film, with its violent and nocturnal moods, minimal sets disguised by low-key lighting and heavy shadows. The '40s became a stimulating time for directors — the explosion of Welles with *Kane* and *The Magnificient Ambersons*, the development of Hitchcock through *Shadow of a Doubt* to *Notorious*, of Cukor through *The Philadelphia Story* to *Gaslight*, the comedies of Preston Sturges, Huston's *The Maltese Falcon* and *We Were Strangers*, the first musicals of Minnelli. Yet Selznick seemed adrift in the period, trying to persuade Margaret Mitchell to write a sequel to *GWTW* or, failing that, something called *The Daughter of Scarlett O'Hara*, and planning a large-scale biography of Hitler to be called, of course, *Mein Kampf*. (Before this project was dropped, he held some conferences on it in elaborately guarded secrecy, and it was always referred to in any correspondence under the code name, *Tales from History*.) He might be one of the few important Hollywood producers openly to admire Welles, but he could never have worked with him, or any other strongly individual director. (While Hitchcock was under contract to him, he did his best work on loan-out.) When Selznick finally returned to movie-making, his reasons were personal.

In 1942 Kay Brown had brought an unknown actress to his attention. He placed her under contract, changed her name from Phyllis Isley to Jennifer Jones, and introduced her to Henry King, who was preparing *The Song of Bernadette* at Fox. She was tested, won the part and later an Academy Award. Deciding to make a Jennifer Jones picture himself, Selznick found a promising part for her in the best-selling novel, *Since You Went Away*, wrote the script, hired a pliable director, John Cromwell, and lined up a glossy surrounding cast — Claudette Colbert, Joseph Cotten, Shirley Temple, Lionel Barrymore, Nazimova, Hattie McDaniel — and his star's husband, Robert Walker. This long and expertly sentimental saga of an American family in wartime betrayed no signs of the tension underlying its making. By the time shooting started, it was clear that Selznick had fallen in love with Jennifer Jones; he was constantly writing new scenes and enlarging others for her, including a love scene played with Walker: another situation that might have come straight from his own *A Star Is Born*. On the screen one saw nothing but showmanship, and the picture was a considerable financial success. He followed it with *Spellbound*, a not very distinguished Hitchcock movie, but again a crowd-pleaser.

His appetite for active production now stimulated again, but his desire for prestige unsatisfied, Selznick began looking around for another super-project. The ghost of *GWTW* no longer seemed friendly — it was malevolent, rather, in the way it set a standard against which everything else would be measured. The time had come to exorcise it. *Since You Went Away* had failed to turn into *SYWA*, but in a novel by Niven Busch, *Duel in the Sun*, he saw the possibilities of making a large-scale western that stood a strong chance of becoming *DITS*.

The movie was prepared and shot following a time of personal and professional crisis. Myron Selznick had recently died; before that, one of his oldest colleagues, Raymond Klune, had left the company. There was a law suit pending (eventually unsuccessful) to prevent Vivien Leigh from appearing on the London stage in *The Skin of Our Teeth*, which he considered unsuitable for her. While the situation with Jennifer Jones was unresolved, a few weeks after *Duel in the Sun* went into production, Irene Selznick decided to end the marriage. Shooting had started in March 1945 with King Vidor as director, again from Selznick's script, but post-production was not completed until the end of 1946, at a cost of about $1,000,000 more than *GWTW*. Complaining of undue interference, Vidor resigned two-thirds of the way through, and the picture was finished by William Dieterle, with a few sequences shot by Josef von Sternberg and the usual multiplicity of second units. Two cameramen were fired before Lee Garmes, in a reversal of the earlier situation, took over. ("Up to his old tricks again," Garmes commented.) The critics' response to this violent, delirious romance between a half-breed (Jennifer Jones) and an outlaw (Gregory Peck) was generally hostile. No *DITS*, its excessive cost also cut into the profits.

For the rest of his life Selznick remained at a crossroads; the more he tried to impose himself, to revive the legend, the less sure his touch seemed. All the remaining productions are scarred by the same kind of disputes, expensively rewritten or reshot; the performer is trembling visibly on the high wire. He personally took over the screenplay of Hitchcock's *The Paradine Case,* and the film ended their association. Like many of the stars, the director decided not to sign a new contract. *Portrait of Jennie,* a tenuous little ghost story, was reshot for months and ended up costing almost as much as *GWTW.* By 1949 the company had gone into liquidation with a bank debt of $12,000,000. Most of its assets — the remaining stars under contract, distribution and television rights to pictures, even the costumes of *GWTW* — were sold. Selznick announced his retirement from picture-making.

After his marriage to Jennifer Jones he found personal happiness again, and agreed, for a while, to play the part of a "respected industry figure," a benign though disenchanted watcher from the sidelines. Then he and his new wife went to Europe, and he made some co-production deals. He raised part of the money for Korda's *The Third Man* and *Gone to Earth,* in return for the American distribution rights, but his active involvement was limited to recutting both movies for the American market and changing the title of the latter to *The Wild Heart.* In Italy he made a similar deal with de Sica on *Terminal Station,* this time obtaining some control of the production. He brought in a succession of writers, changed the title to *Indiscretions of an American Wife.* It was not a success.

Back in Hollywood, he found the ghost beginning to haunt him again, and in 1957 made one last effort to exorcise it. Embarking on a remake of *A Farewell to Arms,* with Jennifer Jones and Rock Hudson, he turned to Ben Hecht for the script.

Memos reflect his hope of recapturing past glory. "Let's really try to do a job that will be remembered as long as *Gone With the Wind,* something that we can be proud of in the years to come." And then, later: "Go to work, and may the god of the movies be with you." He signed John Huston to direct, though an early memo to him in cable expressed the usual misgivings: "I AM PERHAPS NOT UNNATURALLY WORRIED LEST UNQUESTIONED EMINENCE OF YOUR PRESENT POSITION WOULD CAUSE YOU TO RESIST AND RESENT FUNCTIONING AS DIRECTOR RATHER THAN DI-RECTOR-PRODUCER."

It did, and Huston was fired ten days after shooting started. His replacement, Charles Vidor, struggled on under continuous bombardment — "We have spent tons of thousands of dollars on irrelevant or secondary material, most of which will not even stay in the picture," etcetera, etcetera — and the work was an immense nervous strain for everyone involved. No *AFTA,* either critically or commercially, it was Selznick's own definitive farewell. He had one more project in the works, *Tender Is the Night,* but sold it to Fox. His hair was white now, and his face had lost its glow. As successful as ever at each manifestation, the ghost continued to haunt him. In 1961, for the Civil War Centenary, MGM restaged the premiere in Atlanta, the theater facade once more made into a semblance of Twelve Oaks. There he met again the two surviving stars, Vivien Leigh and Olivia de Havilland, and the Champion of Champion Producers took his bow to the old applause.

It stimulated him to a last, wistful project, never realized: a stage musical based on *GWTW.* If there is no way to conquer the past, go directly back to it. Naturally he wanted only the most eminent composers and writers; but they eluded him, fearing comparison with the original. He gave up the idea after a year. The first stage version was presented after his death in Tokyo in 1966, then another one opened in London in 1972,

with a score by Harold Rome and a libretto by Horton Foote. June Ritchie played Scarlett, with Harve Presnell as Rhett. Lavish production effects made it an instant popular success, but the story was hopelessly scrambled and the music undistinguished. There was a "Tara" ballad, of course, and Scarlett sang "Tomorrow Is Another Day," and, with Rhett, "Two of a Kind." It's as well that Selznick didn't live to see it.

I came to know him in the last five years of his life, and was invited to the parties that he and Jennifer gave. They were the largest, grandest, and most civilized social functions in Hollywood, and you could see there many of the colleagues with whom he'd had disagreements, George Cukor and King Vidor, all friends again. When you confronted his personal charm, it was completely understandable. A passionate host, he had an aura of intense personal good will. Although he still toyed with an occasional project, commissioning Christopher Isherwood to write a treatment of the life of Mary Magdalene, wondering if he could obtain the rights to E. M. Forster's A *Passage to India* (he couldn't), his interest in movie-making seemed little more than a reflex, a flicker. "Hollywood's like Egypt," he told Ben Hecht as the two disenchanted survivors strolled the empty streets at dawn, "full of crumbled pyramids. It'll never come back. . . . there might have been good movies if there had been no movie industry. Hollywood might have become the center of a new human expression if it hadn't been grabbed by a little group of book-keepers." Unconsciously, perhaps, he was replaying the role of neglected artist in which he and Myron had cast their father. Perhaps politics interested him more now. Ever since his friendship with Henry Luce in the '40s he had thought of moving into that arena, and he used to say he would have liked to be appointed Ambassador to Moscow. "They need," he stated wryly, "a Jew." He showed no bitterness and retained his impressive grand manner to the end; there was only,

215

at moments, a lost and proudly discouraged quality about him, as with exiled royalty.

In 1959 he had seen the last tangible remnants of his empire disappear when the set of Tara was finally dismantled and shipped for permanent exhibition in Atlanta. It was another moment for exalted and melancholy reflection. "Once photographed, life here is ended. It is almost symbolic of Hollywood. Tara had no rooms inside. It was just a facade." The O, the Omega, confronted him. There was nothing left to do except become, like his most famous work, a monument.

He died from a heart attack on June 22, 1965, aged sixty-three, and was buried at Forest Lawn. At the funeral, Katharine Hepburn recited Kipling's "If" . . .

In her professional life Vivien Leigh exorcised the ghost of *GWTW* by her triumph in the movie of *A Streetcar Named Desire*, for which she won another Oscar; she also did some remarkable work on the stage. Yet, as with Selznick and Gable and Leslie Howard, her later years were ill-omened. The tubercular patch on her lung first appeared when she was playing *The Skin of Our Teeth*, and from then on there were periods of rest under doctor's orders, sometimes lasting more than six months. In 1954, after starting the movie *Elephant Walk* in Hollywood, she had a nervous collapse and was replaced by Elizabeth Taylor. A few years later the marriage with Olivier ended, something from which she never really recovered.

I first met her in 1960, when I was writing the screenplay for *The Roman Spring of Mrs. Stone*. On the professional level, I was struck by the fact that, although she always preferred the stage to the screen, she had an uncanny instinct for movie acting, a true camera sense. She knew exactly how to minimize her effects for a close-up, how to enlarge them for a longer shot, as if the camera for her were some kind of magic mirror in which she could always obtain the desired reflection. Several years later, after her death, I first saw her tests for GWTW, and though her immediate grasp of the character was still astonishing, her technique was not. I had seen it in action and witnessed its light but intense precision. On the personal level, her mixture of elegance and wildness intensified as she grew older. Her flair for clothes and houses, the impeccable food, wine, and flowers when she entertained, were not just "taste." They implied the need for an outward order because inwardly there was a streak of chaos. From the time of her first breakdown, she took shock treatment when she felt a crisis approaching. Before we started shooting *Mrs. Stone* she felt herself going "dry," and with a matter-of-fact calm told the director, Jose Quintero, and myself that she'd better have a "treatment," making it sound no more drastic than taking a couple of aspirin. When she came to Hollywood to make her last film, *Ship of Fools* — another vivid portrait of a southern lady, exquisitely on the skids — she wanted to see not only old friends but new places. She'd heard of a bizarre waterfront bar near Santa Monica and insisted on being taken there. Something in her nature responded to the outrageous and the outcast. Her humor was sharp and frequently bawdy, but she wasn't witty, she was comic — which is the difference between a funny remark and a view of life, for the keenest comic sense always has something desperate behind it. Asked by an interviewer how she increased her emotional range as an actress, she told him in one crisp, loaded word: "Life!"

Before she died of tuberculosis in 1967, at the age of fifty-four, she appeared on the stage in a part she'd always wanted to play, *Lady of the Camellias*. Irony or premonition? Knowing her romantic instincts, one suspects the latter. During the final illness she had to withdraw from rehearsals for Albee's *A Delicate Balance*, the title of which provides her best epitaph.

Returning to wartime England and setting up his own production company after *Intermezzo*, Leslie Howard realized his ambition to direct (*Pimpernel Smith*, *The First of the Few*) before an airliner in which he was traveling from Lisbon to London was shot down by German planes. He was fifty-three. A year before, Carole Lombard had died in a plane crash at the age of thirty-six. For Gable, it was a loss that colored the rest of his life, even though his final marriage was happy. He joined the Air Force, becoming a captain, and went on bombing missions over Germany as a rear gunner. People who knew him at this time found him angry and suicidal. He returned to movies in 1945 with a mediocre picture, *Adventure*, directed by his old friend Victor Fleming — its slogan, "Gable's back and Garson's got him," being the most memorable thing about it.

For the remaining fifteen years of his career, his popular reputation was undimmed, and he became affectionately known as "The King," but a spark seemed lacking behind the famous assurance. None of the films he made was of more than average quality except for his last, *The Misfits*. He died of a heart attack soon after it was finished, aged fifty-nine. The myth that he had become was too powerful to be extinguished by anything except death — though movies like *Teacher's Pet* and *But Not for Me* would have obliterated lesser figures — but Gable was visibly growing tired of it. In a role in *Band of Angels*, obviously based on Rhett Butler, he seemed remote and flat. Increasingly reluctant to work, he raised his price in the hope that nobody would pay it. Perhaps, like Rhett at the end of GWTW, he was gradually surrendering to nostalgia, to the appeal of the "old life" that, as Selznick found, was becoming submerged for ever. His employer of more than twenty years, Louis B. Mayer, died three years before him, stripped of his power at MGM. Cracks had begun to appear in the structure of all the major studios, and Gable departed just as so many people's time was running out.

In Olivia de Havilland's case, Melanie gave great impetus to her future. Although obliged to return to Warners' until her seven-year contract expired, she was dissatisfied with the roles the studio offered her; taking her employers to court when they tried to extend her contract by invoking an option clause, she won her freedom. Until the end of the '50s she enjoyed an active freelance career, with two Academy Awards, for *To Each His Own* and *The Heiress*. For many years she has lived in Paris, vociferously out of sympathy with the "new" Hollywood, but shrewdly avoiding — unlike many stars of her generation — the humiliation of riding a motorcycle or going berserk with an ax in a B picture.

Of the directors, Fleming went on to make only a handful of films, and only one, *Dr. Jekyll and Mr. Hyde,* with Spencer Tracy and Ingrid Bergman, had much vitality. He died in 1949, aged sixty-five, shortly after the expensive failure of his final picture, *Joan of Arc.* In the same year Sam Wood also died, at the same age, after a more prolific career. Working with Cameron Menzies, or a cameraman like James Wong Howe (who remarked succinctly, after *Kings' Row,* "He knew nothing about visuals"), his basic lack of imagination could be disguised. Not, however, his temperament; this usually mild-mannered and affable man exploded into a ferocious right-winger, supported McCarthy's campaign to wipe out Hollywood "Reds," and founded a paranoiac organization called The Motion Picture Alliance for the Preservation of American Ideals.

In retrospect, it appears as if Cukor's dismissal from GWTW was an unknowing escape. His career developed richly. Almost immediately after leaving the picture, MGM assigned him to

The Women, from which Lubitsch had been removed during the preparatory stages. In supporting parts, Cukor cast two unsuccessful contenders for Scarlett, Paulette Goddard and Joan Fontaine. A brief but telling scene established Fontaine as an actress for the first time; ironically, it won her a contract with Selznick. She went on to work with Hitchcock on *Rebecca,* while Cukor resumed his partnership with Katharine Hepburn on *The Philadelphia Story.* Thirty years later he is still vigorously active, having most recently completed a film of Graham Greene's *Travels With My Aunt.*

A last footnote provides a curious link in the chain. Irene Selznick, after her divorce from David, became a successful Broadway producer. She began with the play that was to provide Vivien Leigh's second great movie role, *A Streetcar Named Desire.*

CREDITS
(as they appear on the screen)

PRODUCTION COMPANY: Selznick International.

DISTRIBUTOR: MGM

PRODUCER: David O. Selznick

DIRECTOR: Victor Fleming

SCREENPLAY: Sidney Howard

PRODUCTION DESIGNER: William Cameron Menzies

PHOTOGRAPHY: Ernest Haller

TECHNICOLOR ASSOCIATES: Ray Rennahan, Wilfrid M. Cline

ART DIRECTOR: Lyle Wheeler

INTERIORS: Joseph B. Platt

COSTUMES: Walter Plunkett

SUPERVISING FILM EDITOR: Hal C. Kern

ASSOCIATE FILM EDITOR: James E. Newcom

MAKE-UP AND HAIR STYLING: Monty Westmore, Hazel Rogers, Ben Nye

MUSICAL SCORE: Max Steiner

SPECIAL PHOTOGRAPHIC EFFECTS: Jack Cosgrove

FIRE EFFECTS: Lee Zavitz

PRODUCTION MANAGER: Raymond Klune

SCENARIO ASSISTANT: Barbara Keon

PRODUCTION CONTINUITY: Lydia Schiller, Connie Earle

SECOND UNIT DIRECTOR: Reeves Eason

ASSISTANT DIRECTOR: Eric Stacey

DANCE DIRECTORS: Frank Floyd, Eddie Prinz

TECHNICOLOR COMPANY SUPERVISION: Natalie Kalmus

SOUND RECORDER: Frank Maher

SCARLETT'S HATS: John Frederics

INTERIOR DECORATION: Edward G. Boyle

HISTORIAN: Wilbur G. Kurtz

TECHNICAL ADVISERS: Susan Myrick, Will Price

RESEARCH: Lillian K. Deighton

Cast

RHETT BUTLER: Clark Gable

SCARLETT O'HARA: Vivien Leigh

ASHLEY WILKES: Leslie Howard

MELANIE HAMILTON: Olivia de Havilland

MAMMY: Hattie McDaniel

GERALD O'HARA: Thomas Mitchell

MRS. O'HARA: Barbara O'Neil

AUNT PITTYPAT HAMILTON: Laura Hope Crews

DOCTOR MEADE: Harry Davenport

BELLE WATLING: Ona Munson

SUELLEN O'HARA: Evelyn Keyes

CARREEN O'HARA: Ann Rutherford

PRISSY: Butterfly McQueen

INDIA WILKES: Alicia Rhett

BIG SAM: Everett Brown

UNCLE PETER: Eddie Anderson

CHARLES HAMILTON: Rand Brooks

FRANK KENNEDY: Carroll Nye

MRS. MERRIWETHER: Jane Darwell

MAYBELLE MERRIWETHER: Mary Anderson

EMMY SLATTERY: Isabel Jewell

JONAS WILKERSON: Victor Jory

RENEGADE: Yakima Canutt

BONNIE BLUE BUTLER: Cammie King

BONNIE'S NURSE: Lillian Kemble Cooper

TOM, A YANKEE CAPTAIN: Ward Bond

THE YANKEE DESERTER: Paul Hurst

BRENT TARLETON: George Reeves

STUART TARLETON: Fred Crane

BIBLIOGRAPHY

Books

Felix Barker, *The Oliviers* (Lippincott, 1953).

John Baxter, *Hollywood in the Thirties* (A. S. Barnes, 1968).

Rudy Behlmer (editor), *Memo from David O. Selznick* (Viking Press, 1972).

S. N. Behrman, *People in a Diary* (Little, Brown, 1972).

Alan Dent, *Vivien Leigh* (Hamish Hamilton, London, 1972).

Finis Farr, *Margaret Mitchell of Atlanta* (William Morrow, 1957).

Richard Griffith, *The Movie Stars* (Doubleday, 1970).

Ben Hecht, *A Child of the Century* (Simon and Schuster, 1954).

Charles Higham, *Hollywood Cameramen* (Indiana University Press, 1970).

John Houseman, *Run-Through* (Simon and Schuster, 1972).

Leslie Ruth Howard, *A Quite Remarkable Father* (Harcourt Brace, 1959).

Gavin Lambert, *On Cukor* (Putnam, 1972).

Aaron Latham, *Crazy Sundays* (Viking Press, 1971).

Frances Marion, *Off with Their Heads!* (Macmillan, 1972).

Margaret Mitchell, *Gone with the Wind* (Macmillan, 1936).

Bob Thomas, *Selznick* (Doubleday, 1970).

Norman Zierold, *The Moguls* (Coward McCann, 1969).

Newspapers and Magazines

Ronald Bryden, *Epic* (*The Observer*, London, January 7, 1968).
Alva Johnston, *The Great Dictator* (*Saturday Evening Post*, May 14, 1942).
John Howard Reid, *The Man Who Made GWTW* (*Films and Filming*, London, December 1967).

Unpublished

Charles Higham, *Interview with Ray Rennahan* (American Film Institute, Louis B. Mayer Oral History Series, 1970).

INDEX